The Quantitative
Analysis of
Social Representations

European Monographs in Social Psychology

Series Editor: Dr Rupert Brown
Centre for the Study of Group Processes
Institute of Social and Applied Psychology
University of Kent at Canterbury
England

This distinguished series, sponsored by the European Association for Experimental Social Psychology, has been relaunched under the editorship of Rupert Brown and published under the Harvester Wheatsheaf imprint. The aim of the series is to publish and promote the highest quality of writing in European social psychology and to encourage publications which approach the field from a wide range of theoretical perspectives. Contents of the books may be applied, theoretical or empirical.

The Quantitative Analysis of Social Representations

Willem Doise, Alain Clémence and Fabio Lorenzi-Cioldi

Translated by Julian Kaneko

HARVESTER
WHEATSHEAF

New York London Toronto Sydney Tokyo Singapore

First published 1993 by
Harvester Wheatsheaf
Campus 400, Maylands Avenue
Hemel Hempstead
Hertfordshire, HP2 7EZ
A division of
Simon & Schuster International Group

© 1993, Willem Doise, Alain Clémence,
Fabio Lorenzi-Cioldi

Typeset in 10 on 12pt Palatino and Optima

Printed and bound in Great Britain by
BPCC Wheatons Ltd, Exeter

British Library Cataloguing in Publication Data

A catalogue record for this book is available
from the British Library

ISBN 0-7450-1347-3 (hbk)
ISBN 0-7450-1348-1(pbk)

1 2 3 4 5   97 96 95 94 93

Contents

Introduction:
Nonconsensual Social Representations

This book is based on a simple idea. Authors of works on social representations (SRs) are often criticized for adhering to a consensual view of
social reality. A simple inspection of the literature shows that many
researchers use automatic data-analysis methods to study SRs. These
methods, such as traditional factor analysis or correspondence factor
analysis, all aim to elucidate organizing principles of *differences* between
individual responses. We will recall this point throughout this book
while showing how these analytic techniques enable us to illustrate and
clarify various dynamics of SRs empirically.

Several of these techniques will therefore be explained in a manner
which, it is hoped, will be comprehensible to readers untrained in this
area. We have no intention of flaunting our technical expertise. That
would only strengthen the impression of *'nouveaux riches'* often given by
users of these methods. The primary aim of this book is to help students
or novice researchers who wish to learn about SR research. We will
expound the general principles of various quantitative data-analysis
techniques from the angle of their usefulness for studying SRs. We will
therefore first summarize the foundations of the theory of SRs.

Theory of Social Representations

One of us (Doise, 1986, 1989a,b, 1990) has repeatedly tried to describe
the main characteristics of SRs and define their concept. By way of introduction, we will recapitulate here the basic ideas developed in his texts.
These ideas were initially worked out by Serge Moscovici (1961) thirty
years ago, but they are still relevant, we believe, as evidenced by many
contemporary studies inspired by them (see Jodelet, 1989, for a list of
recent publications).

The theory of SRs had been built around the notions of system and

1

metasystem long before systemic thinking came into vogue. While studying the SRs of psychoanalysis, Moscovici (1961) had observed a number of similarities between the characteristics of adult thinking and those of infantile thinking. Both adults and children use fragmentary information, draw over-general conclusions from specific observations, give greater importance to conclusions than to premises, base arguments of causality on evaluative associations and resort to many redundancies that are both lexical and syntactical. Intrigued by these similarities, Moscovici (1976, 284) pondered the links between infantile thinking and the cognitive characteristics of SRs:

> Is the cognitive system of SRs just as we have seen it because our reason conceals mental organizations peculiar to our earlier age? Or is it the way it is because it corresponds to a collective situation and interaction to which it is adapted? Basically, it could be shown that there is no contradiction.

Actually, both infantile thinking and adult thinking involve two cognitive systems that account for their common characteristics:

> . . . we see two cognitive systems at work: one of them is an operating system that performs associations, inclusions, discriminations and deductions, while the other controls, verifies and selects by means of rules, whether these are logical or not. The latter is a sort of metasystem that re-treats the material produced by the former. (Moscovici, 1976, 254)

The study of SRs consists of analyzing the regulations carried out by the social metasystem in the cognitive system, as far as their links with specific positions in a set of social relationships are clarified. The organizing principles of the metasystem vary with these positions. These principles may, for instance, require strict application of logical principles in a scientific work or aim primarily to defend the cohesion of a group in the event of a conflict with another group. In both cases, cognitive functioning, as understood generally or by authors of works on social cognition (see Moscovici, 1986; Doise, 1989b), is governed by various social regulations, i.e. 'normative regulations that control, verify and direct' (to use Moscovici's words, 1976) cognitive operations.

It is in the second part of Moscovici's (1976) book on social representations of psychoanalysis that one finds, from our point of view, the best example of a study on the insertion of cognitive functioning within the organization of symbolic relationships between social actors. The general aim of the book being the study of the transformation of a scientific theory into common sense, the second part bears more specifically on the way the French press of the 1950s treated psychoanalysis.

Three kinds of publications were analyzed: the press related to the

Communist Party, the press related to the Catholic Church and newspapers with large circulations. These three sectors of the French press had widely varying relationships with their readers and with their social and cultural environment. Therefore, three different communicative relationships were described.

The *diffusion* was characterized by a lack of differentiation between the source and the receivers of the communication. In journals with a large audience, journalists passed on information which they had usually themselves received from specialists. Their principal aim was to disseminate knowledge widely while retaining the interest of their readers. The *propagation* as a form of communication was established by members of a group who relied on a well-organized world vision, who had a belief to propagate, and who aimed to reconcile the contents of other doctrines with their own well-established system. In the example chosen by Moscovici, the question under study was how journals emanating from the Catholic Church reconciled psychoanalytical knowledge with the principles of religion. *Propaganda* was a form of communication embedded in conflicting social relations. The overriding aim of the communication was clearly to differentiate between truth and fiction, to entertain a conflict, an incompatibility between the source's own vision and the mystified vision attributed to the defenders of psychoanalysis.

The cognitive organizations of messages in various communication modalities were different. In the diffusion communicative relationship, themes were not strongly integrated, given standpoints could be different and sometimes contradictory. Depending on the case, psychoanalysis was treated seriously, with reserve or even irony, and was often associated with other fashionable subjects. Without necessarily looking for change in behaviour, a new subject was put in fashion while accepting the fact that opinions on it could differ.

Propagation was characterized by a more complex organization of contents. Catholic writings on psychoanalysis advocated moderation and prudence, while envisaging its use in educational settings. Whereas the notion of libido was dispelled as a general explanatory concept, affectivity was attributed a positive role especially in educational and therapeutic practices. Nevertheless, in contrast to positivism, psychoanalysis was considered to elaborate a more integrated comprehension of the human being as it afforded an important place to symbolism, which could further a revival of a spiritualist vision. Therefore, neither global acceptance nor global disproof of psychoanalysis was advised, some of its ideas being assimilated into the religious message.

The propaganda, on the contrary, recommended universal rejection of a rival conception. In the Communist newspapers of the Cold War period, psychoanalysis was considered as nothing but a pseudo-science imported into France from the USA. Systematic oppositions in society and in politics were related to oppositions in psychology. The Soviet Union was presented as the country of peace, the USA as the country of war and social exploitation. According to such propaganda, the Soviets had developed an heuristically and scientifically valid psychology, whereas the Americans proposed a psychoanalysis which seemed to be scientific in appearance but which, in reality, reflected a mystifying ideology.

Of course, the current representations of psychoanalysis have changed. Moscovici (1976), in a new edition of his book, demonstrates this for the Communist press, where contemporary articles on psychoanalysis reveal propagation, rather than propaganda dynamics. But the general conclusion of Moscovici (1976, 497) remains valid when he proposes an integrative framework for research on opinions, attitudes and stereotypes:

> Considering from the angle of structure of messages, elaboration of social models, relation between senders and receivers, behavioral aims, the three systems of communication maintain their singularity. Therefore, it is specifically their particularity that allows us to link term to term diffusion, propagation and propaganda to opinion, attitude and stereotype.

This conclusion is important: it implies, above all, that definitions of social representations in terms of consensus are insufficient. Only stereotypes are considered to be consensually shared within a given group or subgroup. As attitudes result from efforts of assimilation into an already complex and varied sociocognitive system, they are subject to many variations; opinions are, by definition, fluctuant and follow momentary fashions. More than consensual beliefs, social representations are therefore organizing principles varied in nature, which do not necessarily consist of shared beliefs, as they may result in different or even opposed positions taken by individuals in relation to common reference points.

The heuristic value of this distinction between opinions, attitudes and stereotypes has unfortunately not yet been acknowledged by most social psychologists. This is surely not a coincidence, because researchers who work at the articulation between systems of communication and systems of cognitive organization are rare. But it is beyond the scope of this book to analyze exhaustively the reasons why social psychologists have neglected the study of the links between symbolic relational dynamics and individual cognitive organizations.

When Thomas and Znaniecki (1918–20) published their studies on the Polish peasant in Europe and the United States, they linked 'objective' characteristics of a collective social way of life, which they called social values, to other 'objective' characteristics observed in individual members of a social group and which were given the name of attitudes.

Attitudes were considered as the psychological side of an objective social reality. But subsequently, measurement of individual differences in attitudes has predominantly interested the inventors of scaling paradigms such as Thurstone and Chave (1929), Likert (1932) or even Guttman (1944) whose names are associated with different ways of measuring attitudes. The sophisticated measurement devices they originated, even if some of them are now considered obsolete or of restricted applicability, launched a conception of attitudes that obscured their main function as a reflection of cultural and social relationships. This obscuration became even more evident when, from the 1950s and 1960s onwards, attitude change was experimentally studied, almost exclusively at an individual level, as a matter of cognitive processes.

Recent studies on SRs, however, urge us to reconsider the role data-analysis techniques and statistical analyses can play in operationalizing the links between collective and cognitive dynamics. As this book will show, many of these studies use such analyses in order to study the social dynamics organizing individual variations in opinions, attitudes and stereotypes. If, historically, the development of quantitative techniques may have individualized these notions, nowadays researchers on social representations invert this trend. The main question we try to answer in this book is therefore about the possible contribution of data-analysis techniques in the study of SRs.

To a number of authors, this contribution seems self-evident and needs no clarification. They do not hesitate to present their works, factor-analyzing responses to opinion- or attitude-survey questionnaires, as studies on SRs. While not wishing to sound censorious, we do not think that all these studies necessarily further our understanding of SRs. Our aim is to unearth the potentials of these analyses for clarifying certain points of the theory of SRs. To achieve this objective, we must first describe the two processes which Moscovici (1961) saw at work in SRs: objectification and anchoring.

Objectification concretizes the abstract. It turns the relational of scientific knowledge into an image of a thing. In the SRs of psychoanalysis, for example, psychic dynamics become complexes, entities or even malformations that can be removed by an expert. The basic notion of the libido – the organizing force of psychic life – disappears. According to those questioned, it becomes simple affectivity, an erotic desire or even sexual intimacy between the psychoanalyzed and the psychoanalyst. The importance of thus elucidating the effects of objectification should not be minimized. According to Roqueplo (1974), any disclosure of scientific findings is accompanied by objectification. Hence the importance of taking it into account in scientific education. In this connection, one may even think that the notions of attitude or cognition, as entities 'coded' into the individual, are themselves the results of objectification because of their widespread use.

For our current purpose, however, it is more important to analyze the social function of objectification. Of course, objectification facilitates communication, which is of the utmost importance for the establishment of social relationships. But objectification facilitates communication by dissociating a concept or a statement from the scientific or ideological conceptual context which gives it its full meaning. It is as if common sense would not tolerate the existence of a link between the elements of knowledge which it assimilates and knowledge systems of another nature.

Anchoring consists of incorporating new elements of knowledge into a network of more familiar categories. Moscovici used this process to describe how the image of psychoanalysis fits into prior systems of classification or typology of people and events. The new social practice of psychoanalysis is classified and named according to the links which it is supposed to have with different social categories such as the rich, artists, unbalanced persons, women and children. Hence the importance of studying this process for those who wish to link the psychological and the sociological together in order to free their research on social attitudes and cognitions from its over-concentration on the individual's psychological organization (see Doise, 1989b). It is essential to study the anchoring of attitudes and cognitions in the distinctive characteristics of the social field that generates them if one wishes to study them as SRs.

Objectification and anchoring are apparently poles apart: objectification aims to create truths obvious to everyone, independent of any social or psychological determinism; anchoring denotes the intervention of such determinisms in their genesis and transformation. For this reason, SR research should not only aim to find common knowledge, but also study the modulations of such knowledge according to its specific involvement in a system of symbolic regulations.

One major problem with SR studies is that their raw material is composed of collections of individual opinions, attitudes or prejudices whose organizing principles (common to groups of individuals) must be pieced together. It is precisely for this reason that it is essential to use the different types of data-analysis methods described in this book. These will be grouped according to their contribution to the study of the concepts expounded in this book, but analyzing the actual use of these techniques will also enable us to enrich the SR theory, especially when treating SRs as organizing principles of variations in positions of different individuals.

Structure of the Book

In each part of this book, we will therefore set forth different analytic techniques and the main working hypotheses that guided us when drawing up the book's plan.

Part One will show that objectification is not only a characteristic of SRs but is also at work in various applications of data analysis. In fact, authors often identify the results of their analyses with direct descriptions of SRs present in a given population. Some authors do not even hesitate to mention graphic representations of SRs while commenting on a figure with the projection of loadings of different items obtained by factor analysis or principal-component analysis. This obviously involves objectifications according to the very idea of the SR theory. SRs are viewed as kinds of mental maps, endowed with a quasi-material existence and peculiar to a given population. Data analyses, notably multi-dimensional scaling, would serve primarily to make these maps from individual responses in which they do not appear so distinctly and in such a refined form.

In our view, descriptions of these objectified representations are a major contribution from statistical analysis. It must be borne in mind, however, that the study of SRs is not confined to the study of objectification. Such a reification would not account for the heterogeneity that generally characterizes SRs. Let us recall, in this connection, the pioneering works of Katz and Braly on stereotypes (1933). The two researchers gave American students a list of dozens of traits and asked them to indicate the five traits that best characterized a given ethnic group. The students were thus asked to describe ten groups.

The main index calculated by the authors was the degree of agreement between subjects in the attribution of the five most typical traits of each ethnic group. More specifically, they calculated the minimum number of traits required to achieve half the responses given by the study population. Let us take a fictitious case of 100 subjects questioned by means of a list of dozens of traits from which they must choose five that best characterize a given ethnic group. Ninety, 85, 75, 60 and 55 respondents respectively agree in attributing the traits v, w, x, y and z to this group, while the 135 other responses are divided into several other traits much less consensually. It therefore suffices to total the responses for the three traits v, w and x for obtaining 250 responses, i.e. half the responses. Consequently, the stereotypicality index is 3. This index indicates a very high level of consensuality, since 2.5 traits are the maximum theoretical index when selecting five traits. In our example, however, this high index coexists with the unquestionable heterogeneity of responses. In any event, it is clear that 10 per cent, 15 per cent and 25 per cent respectively of respondents do not consider that the three traits selected are part of the stereotype. The best stereotypicality indices obtained by Katz and Braly from American students were about 4.6 for the image of Blacks, 5.0 for that of Germans and 5.5 for that of Jews. In other words, a relatively high degree of heterogeneity characterizes even responses regarded as very stereotyped (see the study of Manz, 1968, for a detailed discussion of this problem).

The above example not only shows the limits of a consensual conception of SRs but should also prompt us to make the most of techniques that enable us to take this inter-individual variety into account. The use of factor-analytic techniques is clearly incompatible with a consensual view of SRs. This is exactly where a paradox lies: the techniques used to obtain common representations are actually based on a study of inter-individual variations. Statistically, these techniques are often inapplicable when there are 100 per cent consensual responses to certain items. To get programs working, these items must be removed without variation in the responses.

In Part Two, we stress the analysis of individual differences, which is, in fact, the main aim of factor analysis. A theoretical study of inter-individual variations in the area of SRs is still an unexplored area. It is as if the primary aim of SR researchers was to show how scattered and varied fragments of opinions can none the less be integrated into a coherent whole. In this sense, useful work has been done, but the very use of analytic techniques obliges us to revert to the problem of inter-individual differences which we will regard essentially as variations in individual positions in relation to common reference points. Showing that SRs are also organizing principles of differences in individual positions is perhaps the most important contribution of the reasoned use of factor analysis.

A study of SRs must therefore take inter-individual differences into account. There are various techniques, however, for also detecting preferential links between response modalities and between these and other characteristics of respondents. In this sense, these techniques are quite useful for studying the anchoring process at work in SRs and, more specifically, in analyzing the connection between SRs and social memberships. In Part Three, we will give a general idea of various techniques that can be of special help in studying such links.

Objectification, organizing principles and anchoring are the key concepts of our theory of SRs. This book will discuss the main quantitative methods used by various authors to study SRs empirically.

For each method commented upon, we then discuss the characteristics that enable it to apprehend aspects of objectification, organizing principles or anchoring at work in SRs. For this reason, we will generally take an illustrative approach. Clearly, we cannot deal here with all of the application conditions and the various mathematical bases of data-analysis techniques discussed in specialized works. Our work should encourage the reader to become more familiar with these techniques and use them to study SRs with full knowledge of the facts. We also hope that specialists in these techniques will find in this book suggestions for expounding their methods from a fresh viewpoint.

PART I

Common Knowledge

Part One will focus on objectification. While this notion denotes a process by which an abstract object – a concept – is transformed into an image or a figurative schema, the majority of empirical studies have called special attention to the product of this transformation. SRs are, in a way, confounded with a hierarchical structure of 'words' or images. It should be noted, however, that such a perspective, reductive though it is, allows us to demonstrate that this scientific apprehension of objectification is a momentum in the process of construction of a reality – a momentum that springs from the formalization of concrete and everyday knowledge and transforms in return this 'naïve' knowledge into a new reality.

Objectification implies cognitive operations such as selecting, categorization and schematization. They produce biases in everyday understanding that were often explained in terms of needs or desires and that, nowadays, are more often analyzed as shortcomings of human cognitive functioning (Nisbett and Ross, 1980). Cognitive biases are viewed as common characteristics of individuals' information processing rooted in processes of stereotyping, distraction, self-favouritism, etc. Much empirical evidence supports such social cognitive explanations of everyday cognitive functioning.

However, individual reasoning is also embedded in a thinking society or, in other words, individual cognitive systems are regulated by social metasystems. Information processing is inserted in patterns of social communication. To process and exchange information, subjects have to share common theories or social representations which have an existence outside the individual head (Moscovici, 1986). According to SR theory, cognitive products result from the intervention of social regulations in common knowledge more often than from imperfect information processing. Notwithstanding these differences in approaches, it is worthwhile to point out attempts of integration between the social cognition and the SR traditions (see Augoustinos and Innes, 1990).

Studies of objectification aim to assess the contents of 'naive' theories that individuals share about events, objects or situations in their social environment. Three main hypotheses orient these studies.

First, it is assumed that people share a limited number of meanings for a specific object. An important task for researchers, therefore, is to determine the entries of this dictionary of meanings. Which words, images, informations are available to and used by individuals who apprehend social events or social objects? This part of the study of SRs primarily concerns the nature of data and the methods of gathering them; we touch upon it as an introduction to the presentation of various analytic methods. Raw data can be different kinds of individual responses as well as products of media, groups or institutions.

A second hypothesis is that the shared contents of SRs are structured. Different kinds of organizations of common knowledge have been envisaged. The simplest structure is a basic dichotomy between two broad categories of contents but more complex organizations are usually defined. Evidencing such organizations is a matter of data analysis and will be dealt with at some length in the next chapters.

Special attention will be paid to the kind of structures that can be investigated by means of the most commonly used techniques. Three such structures will be discussed. The first one results from a refinement of the idea of a dichotomous classification in terms of similarity or dissimilarity. In this sense, SR's organization is presented as a hierarchical classification based on the degree of similarity between contents. A second type of study stems from the idea that the contents are organized around a few dimensions. Symbolic materials are conceived as distributed on dimensions linking contrasted meanings. The structure is no longer thought of as a tree with hierarchical levels of classification but as a mapping of distances between meanings. Complexity of this structure is reflected in the number of dimensions used to map out the data, more dimensions are needed when differentiations happen to be less consensual. The third form of structure is grounded on the same idea of a map. But in this map elements of meaning are arranged according to the degree with which their relationships deviate from the average relationships between all elements. Complexity of the structure is determined by the number of axes needed to account for the pattern of such deviations.

The third hypothesis assumes that the structure of a SR is oriented by a few attitudinal dimensions. Each element of a representation not only has a meaning but an evaluative connotation as well that is widely accepted by people of the same social world. Orientation of the structure can be defined by interpreting the different clusters, dimensions or axes. Another possibility is to determine the orientation by weighting the data according to subjects' judgements. This aspect will lead us to report briefly on the use of attitude scales, and on Osgood's scale in particular, for defining orientations of a structure.

For many researchers, a SRs structure is organized around a nucleus or a core which constitutes the stable and meaningful linkage of all the SR's elements. In this sense, such a core is comparable to a schema (see Augoustinos and Innes, 1990). This view implies to some extent that such a structure is objectified in an internal, psychological structure shared by individuals in a same social world. The question is about the links between a statistical representation of data and their psychological organization. We address this point at the end of Part One.

But let us state here that the existence of SRs is without doubt objectified and crystallized in different symbolic and material institutions of the society (e.g. legal rules and norms, etc). If individuals take part in a common structure, this may merely imply that they refer to the same institutionalized systems of meanings. However, in Part Two we emphasize that individuals position themselves differently in relation to such common systems of meanings and that they can accentuate or weaken links that are objectified in a SR. Hence, their individual representations do not necessarily espouse the objectified structure of a common representation.

1

Automatic Cluster Analysis:
Proximities between Contents of a Social Representation

SR studies involve linguistic material such as responses to question-naires, free associations of words and conversations. This fact has inevitably led to fierce debates over the relevance of statistical and theo-retical methods used to treat such data. The disputes are, of course, all the more heated as they concern discourses culled from conversations, for instance, and we are dealing here not only with semantic indicators but also with syntactic structures. We are talking about material whose treatment does not preclude this kind of debate.

We will study, primarily but not exclusively, the data obtained by standardized or semi-standardized questionings. Most works on SRs often begin with open investigations that enable semantic universes to be defined. One of the most commonly used techniques is the free asso-ciation of words (see De Rosa, 1988, and Le Bouedec, 1984).

Initially used in an individualistic perspective, free association of words was adapted by social-psychologists as a means to identify shared conceptions of widely used notions such as intelligence, work, health and sickness. The way they proceed in treating such associations results in an objectification of a consensual apprehension of reality. Differences between individuals or between groups are rarely taken into consideration as evidenced in the examples we will present in this part of the book. Parts Two and Three will develop our views on the analysis of inter-individual and inter-group variations in the study of SRs.

The material thus obtained can be put together in a collection of words used by the whole study population, one of its groups or each individual. Such collections are called dictionaries amenable to various types of treatment. Generally, there are two ways of treating this kind of material. The first consists of directly using the 'words' to reveal uni-verses common to different stimuli. In the second type of treatment, the 'words' are used more to define their organization and apprehend a 'deeper' structure of the SR field. We will begin by briefly describing a study on the treatment of dictionaries by the first approach. This will give us the opportunity to introduce multivariate hierarchical cluster analysis, which we will then discuss in greater detail.

Hierarchical Cluster Analysis of Word Associations

To define the semantic universe of a SR, it may be useful to obtain, using a word-association technique, information on words that are known to be used to image the object of representation. These words can be defined by their links between themselves and with the represented object. This may involve links of similarity or difference or various implicative relationships. A comparison of the dictionaries obtained for each of the words then enables us to specify a representational field and its relationships with closely related fields. This operation can be performed for the whole study population without taking account of individual variations in the number and nature of associated words. It is generally admitted, implicitly or not, that there is a single SR of the object or at least a solid basis common to all individuals.

Illustration: A Protest Movement

Di Giacomo (1980) studied the SRs of a protest movement led by students at the Catholic University of Louvain, Belgium. Among other measures, the author selected nine stimulus words to define and compare semantic universes close to, or distant from, the movement. The stimulus words apt to characterize the movement were: the *committee* against the 10 000 (name given to the committee that organized the protest movement against the Belgian Government's decision to double university enrolment fees from 5000 to 10 000 Belgian francs), *strike* (suggested by the committee), *extreme left* (the committee's political leanings) and *workers* (because of the committee's appeal to student–worker solidarity). As opposed to them, the following words were suggested: *power* (against which the movement was directed), *extreme right* (opposed to the committee's extreme leftism), *executives* (in opposition to workers) and the *AGL* (the General Assembly of the Students of Louvain which took over the movement). The word *students* (group wooed by the committee and the AGL) may be considered the 'hinge' word: the author wanted to know if the students were perceived to be in the sphere of influence of the committee or the AGL. Each of the 281 questioned subjects was asked to associate as many words as he/she wished with one of the nine words.

Since the total number of different words used was large (977 for 1631 words), it was more than halved (to 453) by aggregating semantically similar words (examples: right-winger – right; I don't know – unknown; Leninist, Trotskyist and Communist – Marxist *sic*). The analyzed material was thus composed of nine dictionaries, each corresponding to a stimulus word, for comparison.

The author first built a similarity matrix between these dictionaries by calculating an index called Ellegard's association index. This index was calculated by dividing the number of words common to two dictionaries by the square root of the product of the words of the two dictionaries. It thus varied between 0 and 1, because the higher the percentage of common words, the higher the index. In the above-mentioned study, the author observed a high similarity index between the *committee* against the 10 000 and *strike* (0.40), while the similarity index between *executives* and *extreme left* was low (0.09). This meant that common words associated with the first two stimulus words were more numerous than those associated with the other two stimulus words.

The similarity matrix was then analyzed by a hierarchical cluster method (see Beauvois, Roulin and Tiberghien, 1990, 197–200, for introduction to this analytic technique). Automatic cluster techniques for finding groups of objects (individuals or responses) that are similar according to certain criteria are particularly effective in revealing structures of representations. Hierarchical cluster analysis (HCA) enabled the author, in the present case, to group words exhibiting the highest degree of similarity between them. A tree diagram or dendrogram (see Figure 1.1) enabled him to visualize the classes thus created and the closeness of the links between their components.

The dendrogram is read as follows: stimuli are assembled according to their decreasing similarity rated on a scale ranging from the left to the right of the diagram. Thus, the already classified groups of stimuli are in turn classified into other groups until all responses are assembled in a single group whose degree of similarity is entered on the right of the diagram. Two stimuli will be aggregated at a level all the more distant in the tree as the classes of which they are members are quite distinct from each other. The final result takes the characteristic shape of a hierarchical cluster tree. This is a hierarchy of groups of stimuli that fit together. To interpret it, one sets an intermediate threshold of distance between groups. This threshold provides a meaning to each assembly of responses. The setting of this threshold does not follow any strict statistical rules: the groups thus obtained should make sense theoretically. Reading these diagrams is then simple. On the Y-axis are the nine stimuli in order of decreasing similarity (thus, *committee*, *strike* and then *AGL* are the closest stimuli). On the X-axis is the degree of similarity between stimuli: the more distant the linkage point, the greater the difference between these stimuli. The author commented on this result as follows:

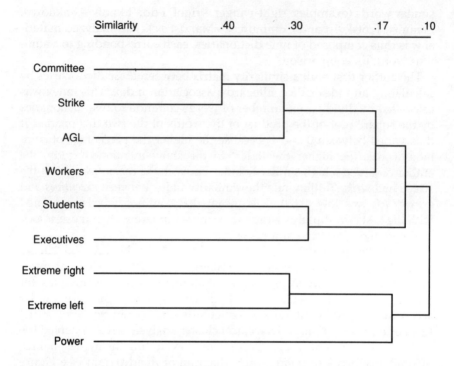

Figure 1.1 *Graphic representation (dendrogram of HCA, complete-link method) of stimulus words used by Di Giacomo (1986) in his study of SRs of a protest movement.*

Note: Different HCA methods (simple-link, complete-link and Ward) are presented below

The first separation in the tree opposes *power, extreme right* and *extreme left* to the other words. It seems that the dictionaries associated with *students, executives, AGL, strike, committee* and *workers* are more similar than words associated with the political field. It appears, therefore, that the SRs of the investigated words are organized primarily on the basis of belonging or not belonging to a 'political' world. The students place themselves in a nonpolitical universe. This universe is next differentiated according to proximity with the students themselves. *Executives* and *students* are soon isolated from the rest. In the 'non-student' branch, *workers* is immediately separated from words having something to do with the '10,000 movement'. (Di Giacomo, 1980, pp. 336–7)

In the above study, HCA of words was to provide an answer to the question: why did the protest movement launched by the *committee* fail?

It was postulated that the structure of this content would reflect oppositions. The method used by the author enabled him, in fact, to distinguish between separate universes: in the present case, it showed that the
semantic field associated with the 'political' was clearly separated from
the rest, including the student protest movement. It was also found that
the dictionary associated with *students*, while close to that associated
with *executives*, had few points in common with the words associated
with the movement and the word *workers*. These results provided a hint
of an answer to the question asked by Di Giacomo. In fact, the word
AGL entered by the author as opposed to the *committee* found itself very
close to the *committee* itself. Moreover, since the movement's failure
must be assessed in the course of time, one may ponder the evolution of
the hierarchical structure thus obtained, which was only a partial and
especially static objectification.

The similarity matrix treated by HCA may be composed of words, as
done by Di Giacomo, or of other forms of verbal production such as
argumentative units or thematic categories. In this case, only the common structure of SRs is studied. The semantic multiplicity introduced by
the questioned individuals can be checked by asking them to associate a
given number of words with the stimulus word or to select words from
a list drawn up in advance. When treating data for the whole population, searching for a common view to that population regarded as a
whole prevails over considering the possible heterogeneity of the population.

Hierarchical Cluster Analysis of Individual Responses

Variables can be grouped differently. Rather than basing an analysis
directly on the presence or absence of common responses in a population, one may first treat individual responses. It would be absurd to perform this operation for word associations such as those analyzed by Di
Giacomo. His subjects, in fact, responded to only one stimulus word and
thus produced only one dictionary. To take this approach, it is necessary
to have several dictionaries or use another questioning technique (for
example, giving subjects a standardized list of words or responses and
asking them to indicate the degree of their similarity to a stimulus
theme). It is then possible first to compare the levels of responses of each
subject or to define similarities and differences between individual
responses. Subsequently, a structure common to individual subjects will
be revealed.

This method is used in many SR studies. Using an example, we will
show what distinguishes HCA based on the mean levels of responses

(calculated for the whole study population) from HCA based on individual levels.

Illustration: Male and Female Identities

In a study of the perception of the ingroup and the outgroup (Lorenzi-Cioldi, 1988b), 240 subjects (120 boys and 120 girls) described men and women in general using a list of twenty-four traits (eight stereotypical male traits, eight stereotypical female traits and eight neutral traits: a subset of characteristics in a questionnaire compiled by Bem in 1974 to measure sex stereotypes). The subjects indicated on a seven-point scale to what degree each trait characterized different targets (1: uncharacteristic; 7: very characteristic). This study dealt with several situations of which only one will be considered in this example. In this situation, the traits were presented as generally differentiating between the sexes. The subjects were asked to describe men and women in general by means of these traits.

Let us consider the responses of ten individuals on six scales (sure of himself, independent, unpredictable, friendly, shy and sensitive) to describe men in general (see Table 1.1). A glance at the means shows that the traits can be grouped in three pairs according to the degree of their relevance to the male image: *sure of himself* and *independent* typically define men, as opposed to *shy* and *sensitive*, while *unpredictable* and *friendly* are used moderately to describe men. When adopting a consensual perspective of SR, only the level of population's responses indicated by the means will be examined. Let us subject the matrix of

Table 1.1 *Responses of ten individuals on six scales describing men in general*

	Sure of himself	Independent	Unpredictable	Friendly	Shy	Sensitive
1	7	7	1	4	1	3
2	6	7	5	4	3	3
3	6	6	7	5	2	1
4	7	5	7	3	4	2
5	7	5	2	4	1	1
6	5	5	3	4	1	2
7	6	7	1	2	2	1
8	5	6	5	5	3	1
9	7	6	1	4	2	3
10	6	6	7	3	1	1
Mean	6.2	6.0	3.9	3.8	2.0	1.8
SD	0.8	0.8	2.6	0.9	1.1	0.9

differences between means to a HCA. To do so, we will transform the differences into Euclidean distances, since this dissimilarity index is commonly used to treat differences between continuous variables. The expression of dissimilarity by a Euclidean distance measurement pre-supposes that inter-item relations can be treated as distances between points of a space. The most commonly used distance coefficient equals the square root of the sum of the squared differences between values associated with two stimuli.

The matrix of dissimilarity between the means is given at Table 1.2. The procedure for obtaining this matrix can be illustrated by an example. The mean difference between *friendly* and *shy* is 1.8 but the distance between these two stimuli is not only this difference, as we have also to consider the differences of these two stimuli with respect to the remaining stimuli (see Kruskal and Wish, 1976, pp. 15–19). Hence, we calculate the Euclidean distance first by adding the six squared differences (all equal to 1.8^2) and second by taking the square root of the sum (SQRT of $19.44 = 4.41$).

It should be noted that the fact of 'squaring' the differences between the values means that the greatest distances are accentuated. Such a pro-cedure is consistent with a psychosocial viewpoint according to which a greater distance is a clearer sign of dissimilarity. HCA enables the tree represented in Figure 1.2 to be built.

HCA confirms the structure identified by the first look at the distances between means.

In reverting to individual data, it was found that score distribution was homogeneous for all items, with the exception of *unpredictable*. Some individuals thought that this trait well characterized the male image, while others disagreed. For the former, *unpredictable* was appar-ently similar to *independent* or *sure of himself*, whereas for the latter, it was similar to *shy* or *sensitive*. By subjecting the matrix of distances between means to a HCA, one totally erased the hetereogeneity intro-duced by individuals and jumped to the conclusion that unpredictable

Table 1.2   *Similarity matrix (Euclidean dissimilarity coefficient matrix) based on the mean relevance of six words for describing the male image*

	Sure of himself	Independent	Unpredictable	Friendly	Shy
Independent	0.49				
Unpredictable	5.63	5.14			
Friendly	5.88	5.39	0.24		
Shy	10.29	9.80	4.65	4.41	
Sensitive	10.78	10.29	5.14	4.90	0.49

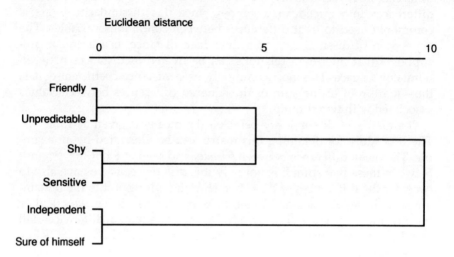

Figure 1.2 *Graphic representation of HCA (complete-link method) of distances between the mean attributions of six descriptive traits of the male image.*

was similar to friendly. To avoid this problem, it was necessary to build a matrix based on differences between individual scores. The procedure consists here of taking the square root of the sum of squared individual differences between two stimuli. For example, the individual differences between *friendly* and *shy* vary from 3 (cases 1, 3, 5 and 6) to –1 (case 4). The square root of the sum of squared differences is equal to 7.07 (SQRT of 50). One thus obtained the following matrix (Table 1.3) which, when subjected to a HCA, led to a grouping of items different (Figure 1.3) from that obtained previously.

It was found that inter-item dissimilarities were higher and that the

Table 1.3 *Similarity matrix (Euclidean dissimilarity coefficient matrix) based on the individual relevance of six words for describing the male image*

	Sure of himself	Independent	Unpredictable	Friendly	Shy
Independent	3.46				
Unpredictable	11.36	11.00			
Friendly	8.60	8.00	7.81		
Shy	13.86	13.27	9.22	7.07	
Sensitive	14.21	13.64	11.27	7.35	4.00

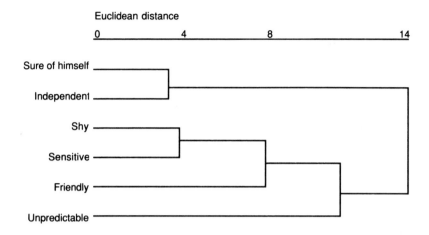

Figure 1.3   *Graphic representation of HCA (complete-link method) of distances between the individual attributions of six descriptive traits of the male image.*

tree made it possible first to distinguish the typical traits from all others. Among the latter, one could then separate *unpredictable* on the one hand from *shy, sensible* and *friendly* on the other. This data representation was more consistent with score distribution in the whole study population than was the representation deduced from the means. This illustration is, of course, very simple. However, it is certainly a straightforward illustration of two different approaches of objectification. The first one emphasizes the consensus and the other takes into account variations in the population. As we have seen, results differ according to each methodological procedure. It appears finally that the latter approach ends up with a richer summary of obtained results and therefore gives a more complex view of objectification.

We can now supplement the results obtained for the male image with the dendrogram obtained by HCA for all traits and subjects for each target. The inter-item distances were calculated from individual scores. Figure 1.4 shows the results obtained for the male image and Figure 1.5 those obtained for the female image.

To make it easier for us to comment on the main results, the groups of traits which we chose for interpretation were numbered in each graph (near the left of the figures). Thus, for example in Figure 1.4, group 2 (*independent, self-confident* and *sure of himself*) is well isolated from groups 3 to 5 and fairly well isolated from group 1, as can be seen at the level where it links up with all these groups.

We will comment on the two trees by comparing the two images that

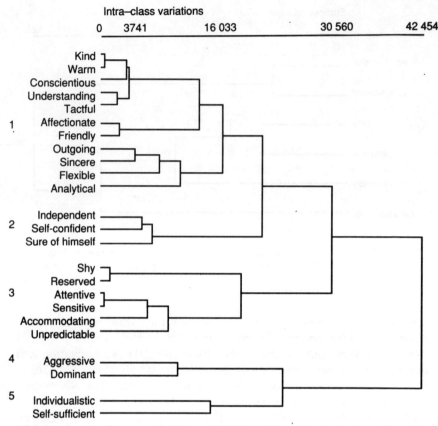

Figure 1.4 *Graphic representation of HCA (Ward's method) of ratings of men in general by subjects of both sexes.*

Note: The classes of traits selected are numbered on the left of the graph. HCA by Ward's method (see below) is based on the comparison of intra- and inter-class variations in Euclidean distances between traits.

may emerge from them. Major differences appear between the descriptions of the two targets (by both boys and girls). By way of illustration, let us consider two traits: *independent* and *individualistic* (stereotypically male traits denoting instrumental autonomy). In any case, these traits form two clearly separate groups probably according to their differential evaluations that are positive for *independent* and negative for *individualistic* (as we found by examining the evaluative judgements given by subjects in this same study). Let us first look at the cluster tree that concerns the male target. The traits considered are associated respectively with those that, like them, represent an autonomous individual. Thus, *independent* is closely associated with *self-confident* and *sure of himself* in

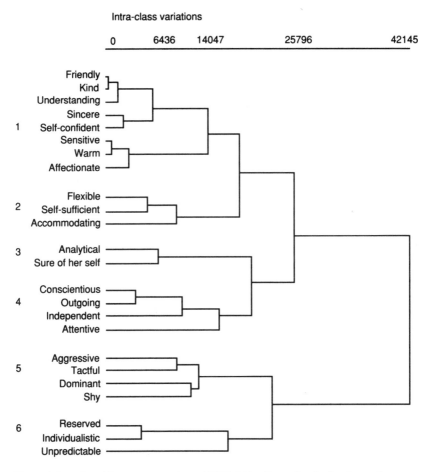

Intra-class variations

Figure 1.5 *Graphic representation of HCA (Ward's method) of ratings of women in general by subjects of both sexes.*

Note: The classes of traits selected are numbered on the left of the graph. HCA by Ward's method (see below) is based on the comparison of intra- and inter-class variations in Euclidean distances between traits.

its assertions (group 2). *Individualistic* is associated with *self-sufficient* and, to a lesser extent, with *aggressive* and *dominant* (groups 4 and 5). The results concerning the links with these traits are, however, quite different when subjects describe the female target. *Independent* (group 4) is associated with *conscientious, outgoing* and *attentive*. *Individualist* (group 6) is associated with *reserved* and *unpredictable*. As shown in Figure 1.5, the idea of personal autonomy or independence has radically different meanings depending on the target of judgement. For the target 'women

in general', this idea seems to be built more in the network of relationships with others. Other traits bear out this interpretation all along the
tree. Thus, for instance, *self-sufficient*, which is associated with *individualistic* for men in general, is associated with *flexible* and *accommodating* for
women. Identical characteristics, linked together in two different ways,
convey different meanings.

This example shows that the study of objectification is not limited to
the study of links between semantic elements considered per se. The
structure of these links depends on the social group to which the semantic universe refers. It is also important to emphasize that the male and
female images highlighted by this analysis are based on specific links
between semantic elements – relations in the relevance level of descriptors for the two images. Other links between these descriptors (correlations, for example) can be apprehended the better to characterize one
and the other. In Part Two, we will deal at greater length with the consideration of individual variations in the analysis of SRs. We will simply
emphasize here that, when pointing up classes of stimuli such as words
and traits to define the organization of the SR field, one should not postulate *a priori* a homogeneous and consensual set of responses within a
population. Taking data heterogeneity into account provides as much
information on the field as does the relationship inferred solely from the
mean levels of responses.

We will now deal with the HCA of dichotomous data. This will lead
us to discuss different similarity coefficients and various HCA models
on the basis of individually calculated similarities.

Similarity Indices and Hierarchical Cluster Analysis

Illustration: Wage Determinants

We will take an example from our study of apprentices in a region of
French-speaking Switzerland. Since we will repeatedly revert to this
research, we will first briefly describe it. It was an opinion survey using
a standardized questionnaire and involving 702 apprentices, aged
between 16 and 20, who were being trained at a manufacturing or craft-
industrial firm while taking theoretical courses at a vocational school.
We studied their perception of different aspects of work and training
(choice of an occupation, sense of work, occupational preferences, relationships with the employer and other apprentices, etc.). The questionnaire was compiled in different forms to permit a differentiated
investigation of a theme (for example, some subjects were to classify in
order of preference the fourteen different apprenticeships offered by
their school, while others were asked to deal with fourteen occupations

difficult of access to this population). It should be noted that, since our hypotheses were based on attribution theories, the subjects were asked to take a definite position on suggested responses evoking large attributional dimensions such as internal causality versus external causality and explanation in terms of causes or reasons (see Béroud, Clémence and Meyer, 1985; Clémence, Deschamps and Roux, 1986; Deschamps and Clémence, 1987). We wish to make it clear that the examples we will give on the basis of this material aim primarily to illustrate the use of a data-treatment technique. Their specific contributions to the study of SRs will have to be rated according to other criteria.

Subjects were asked to indicate what determines a worker's wages by checking off the answer(s) that were closest to their opinion. The suggested items were: his *performance*, his *marital status*, his *responsibilities*, his *training*, the *cost of living*, his *hierarchical level*, his *employer*, his *length of service*, his *company*, the *sector* in which he works and his *political ideas*.

The above question was put to 185 subjects. Four of them failed to answer and were excluded from our analyses. In addition, seven subjects gave an answer other than those suggested.

We wish to show how the answers to such a question can be treated to reveal the way they are linked together by individuals and to extract a structure that enables the responses to be organized. We propose building such a field from the co-occurrences of individual responses on five items in order the better to clarify our purpose. Co-occurrences are defined as the number of individuals who checked off two items at the same time. Table 1.4 shows the matrix of co-occurrences of individual responses between the five items retained and the total frequency of choices of each item.

The above matrix reveals a close association between *performance* and *responsibility* and weak links between *hierarchy* and other items. However, it is easy to see that this matrix has the drawback of giving excessive weight to the frequency of occurrences of an item. For

Table 1.4   *Number of subjects who checked off two items (co-occurrent responses) as wage determinants*

Items	Performance	Responsibility	Marital status	Inflation	hierarchy
Responsibility	68				
Marital status	40	35			
Inflation	43	40	32		
Hierarchy	18	17	10	7	
Total	105	100	62	68	25

Note: Total is the number of subjects who choiced each item. See the text for full-wording items. The respondents numbered 181.

instance, co-occurrences between *performance* and *responsibility* appear to be more than twice co-occurrences between *marital status* and *inflation*. Does this mean that *performance* and *responsibility* are linked together more closely than *marital status* and *inflation*? No. Co-occurrences between the two latter items would be maximum sixty-two if all subjects who checked off *marital status* had also chosen *inflation*. It is clear that *marital status* would have been, in this case, more closely linked together by the subjects than *performance* and *responsibility* even if co-occurrences between these latter ones are still more frequent. Strong association between *performance* and *responsibility* was then due, at least partially, to the fact that they were cited more often by subjects than *marital status* and *inflation*. To take this point into account, we will transform this matrix by relating the co-occurrences between two items to the number of subjects who checked at least one of the two items. Table 1.5 shows the matrix obtained by the transformation. Let us look at the above example to indicate how the new indices are calculated. *Inflation* and *marital status* are both mentioned by 32 subjects; 36 others subjects (=68–32) cited also the item *inflation* and 30 (=62–32) the item *marital status*. Then, 98 subjects (=32+36+30) checked off at least one of the two items. We thus obtain a similarity index of 0.327 (=32/98) between *inflation* and *marital status*. Between *performance* and *responsibility* the similarity index is 0.496. Such an index is called a simple similarity index or Jaccard's similarity index.

This matrix can now be subjected to a HCA. There are different types of HCA. Let us take the one considered simplest and easiest to use: 'simple- or minimal-link' analysis. The principle of this analysis is to consider similarities between pairs of items. As in any HCA, the highest similarity index will be used as the point of departure, thereby creating a first grouping (here between *performance* and *responsibility*). The most important index is then considered (here between *performance* and *inflation*). If one of the items is already in the existing group, the second item is added to this group (the item *inflation* is therefore added to the group composed of *responsibility* and *performance*). Otherwise, a new class is created.

Table 1.5　*Jaccard's similarity indices between five wage determinants*

Items	Performance	Responsibility	Marital status	Inflation
Responsibility	<u>0.496</u>			
Marital status	0.315	0.276		
Inflation	<u>0.331</u>	0.313	<u>0.327</u>	
Hierarchy	<u>0.161</u>	0.157	0.130	0.081

Note: The underlined indices are those selected by HCA to group the items.

In our example, at the last stage of classification, one notices that the results contain only two classes: one includes all items except *hierarchy* which forms the second class all by itself. Figure 1.6 shows the results of the analysis.

The results obtained are rather disappointing. For one thing, the dendrogram shows only one grouping (or more precisely, a group composed of four items and a group composed of the item *hierarchy* alone), and, for another, the items join together in an order well predicted by the classification of the percentage of co-occurrences. These trivial results are due to two elements that add up. The first element stems from the selected similarity index that gives a lot of weight to the frequency with which each item was cited by noting only the similarity between choices. The second is due to the type of HCA that induces a so-called chaining effect. The simple grouping criterion leads almost inevitably to the linking together of items because co-occurrence of one of the items already entered into the analysis with a remaining item is likely to be higher than co-occurrences among remaining items.

It is then possible to choose a similarity index that also takes into account the subjects who mentioned neither of the two items. This index, called a paired similarity index, is calculated by taking into account the number of times two items are accepted or rejected by the same individuals. Reverting to the items *marital status* and *inflation*, one finds that 115 subjects either accepted or rejected both items. In relation to the total number of subjects concerned (all respondents), one obtains a paired similarity index of 0.64. As shown in Table 1.6, these similarity indices are clearly higher than those obtained on the sole basis of item

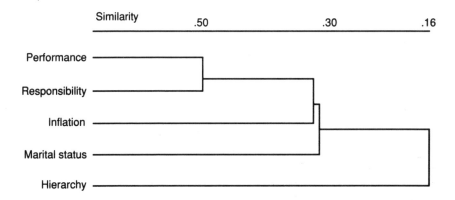

Figure 1.6   *Graphic representation of HCA (simple-link method) of wage determinants, based on the simple similarity matrix.*

Table 1.6   *Indices of paired similarity between wage determinants*

Items	Performance	Responsibility	Marital status	Inflation
Responsibility	<u>0.619</u>			
Marital status	<u>0.519</u>	0.492		
Inflation	0.519	0.514	<u>0.635</u>	
Hierarchy	0.481	0.497	<u>0.630</u>	0.564

Note: The underlined indices are those selected by HCA to group the items.

acceptance. One also notices that the weight of levels (i.e. the frequency of choices of each item) is further minimized.

The dendrogram built on the basis of these coefficients by the 'simple-link' method of HCA is shown by Figure 1.7.

The results thus obtained are appreciably different from the preceding ones. The order of inclusion of the items in the groupings is thus completely modified. The similarity coefficient used enables us to strengthen the link between less chosen items (such as *inflation* and *marital status*) and to separate non-overlapping items more clearly. Thus, the dendrogram shows two large groupings (*responsibility* and *performance* for one and *marital status, inflation* and *hierarchy* for the other). This difference stems from the fact that the highest similarity coefficient appearing after that between *marital status* and *hierarchy* (this latter being entered into the first group) is the similarity coefficient between *performance* and *responsibility*. It is therefore necessary to create a new grouping at this proximity level. The chaining effect is thus broken.

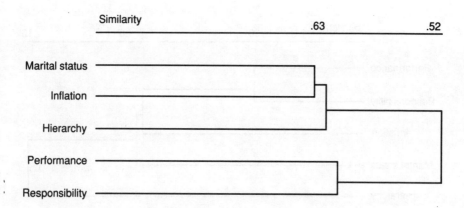

Figure 1.7   *Graphic representation of HCA (simple-link method) of wage determinants, based on the paired similarity matrix.*

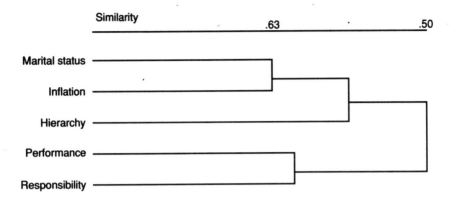

Figure 1.8   *Graphic representation of HCA (complete-link method) of wage determinants, based on the paired similarity matrix.*

How to interpret the two sets of responses obtained by this analysis? On the one hand, one finds the most frequently cited items (*performance* and *responsibility*) that can be interpreted as making the worker's wages dependent primarily on his individual contribution to production. On the other hand, the order in which the items are grouped is linked to the frequency of their reduced acceptance. These items differ from the former in that they presuppose the mediation of the social context more and stress the subject's own will less. This interpretation however, would have to be corroborated by other findings.

By the complete- or maximum-link method of HCA, one generally obtains more distinct groups of items than by the simple-link method. To integrate a new item into a group by this new method, it is no longer enough if the link between one of the already grouped items and another item is closer than all other inter-item links. In fact, it is also necessary to consider the links between this new item and all of the already grouped items. The new item can be linked to the existing group only if all these links are closer than the other links. Otherwise, one forms a new group with the remaining two items exhibiting the closest link between them. In our example, the analysis creates a first group as previously by selecting the two closest items (*marital status* and *inflation*). One then finds that the similarity coefficient between *hierarchy* and *marital status* is the highest (0.63), but *hierarchy* is less close to *inflation* (0.56) than *performance* is to *responsibility* (0.61). Consequently, a group comprising these latter two items will be created before linking *hierarchy* to *marital status* and *inflation*. The dendrogram is shown in Figure 1.8.

The dendrogram thus obtained is relatively close to the preceding one. By cutting the tree at the similarity coefficient of 0.60, however, one obtains three groups of wage determinants, since *hierarchy* forms a group all by itself. In the end, the analysis reveals a structure composed of three groups that seem to correspond to references or separate analyses of society. For one thing, it would seem that subjects gave greater importance to the worker's own will when mentioning *performance* and *responsibility*. For another, they appear to have been guided more by relational and social logic, since the economic component and its variables (*inflation* and *marital status*) are separated from a more structural and stable component (*hierarchy*).

As mentioned above, however, it should be noted that this interpretation must be taken with caution. One should also wonder at this stage what similarity index should be chosen to treat such responses. The coefficient based on both the acceptance and rejection of items presupposes that, for subjects, the fact of checking off an item is equivalent to the fact of ignoring it. This postulate is doubtful. The simple similarity index (based on item acceptance) seems better suited for treating the material considered in this example than the paired similarity coefficient which is more relevant when subjects must explicitly indicate that they accept or reject a suggestion. This coefficient is none the less very useful for comparing items whose acceptance and rejection levels are high.

Let us point out that one can use HCA methods other than the 'simple-link' or 'complete-link' method. The 'Ward' and 'mean-link' methods are based on the mean proximity between items. The 'Ward' method, of which an example has been given above, aims to maximize group homogeneity. In this case, an item is linked to an existing group if the increase in variance it causes remains smaller than that between this item and another item (or another group of items).

We have just shown that HCA can be used on different data matrices that are built on proximity relations between stimulus words. We have illustrated only a small part of the existing types of proximity index or cluster analysis. The reader will find detailed discussions on this subject in more specialized works (e.g. Hudson, 1982; Aldenderfer and Blashfield, 1985).

Similarity Analysis

Flament (1986) proposed another way of classifying words based on a similarity coefficient. His similarity analysis method can be briefly defined as follows: 'It is generally admitted that two items will be all the closer in representation as a larger number of subjects treat them in the same way (by either accepting or rejecting both items). One calculates a contingency coefficient which is a classic similarity index' (Flament, 1986, 141). One thus obtains a similarity matrix comparable to that based on the paired similarity index that can be simplified by searching for the maximum tree of the system. This notion flows from the graph theory and denotes a 'connected and cycleless' graph, i.e., a graph in which all elements (forming the summits of the graph) are linked together and there is only one way to go from one element to another.

Illustration: Game and Problem Solving

Here is an example taken by Flament from Abric and Vacherot (1976). It was a study of the representation of a 'prisoner's dilemma'-type task that may be perceived as a game situation or a problem-solving situation. The authors chose twenty-six words from a pre-survey referring to one or the other of these situations. They then asked subjects who had performed a prisoner's dilemma-type task to choose from among the twenty-six words those that evoked the situation in which they found themselves. The maximum tree of the similarity system (comprising 325 correlations) is represented in Figure 1.9 where each word represents a summit. The similarity indices are indicated along the links between summits (or crests). Such a tree is built as follows.

First, the crests are arranged according to the decreasing value of the similarity index associated with them. One then selects the first two crests that will necessarily be part of the maximum tree because they cannot be the smallest in any cycle. To these first two crests, one adds any crest that does not form a cycle with those already chosen. The crests thus chosen in the maximum tree are those that are not minimum in any cycle (see Degenne and Vergès, 1973). To illustrate this, let us take the example of the elements *Luck, Chance* and *Casino* that appear in the above maximum tree. The crests (*Luck* and *Chance*) and (*Casino* and *Chance*) are entered on the graph and are worth 0.50 and 0.36 respectively. One therefore infers that the crest (*Luck* and *Casino*) is smaller than 0.36. If such was not the case, the crest (*Casino* and *Chance*) would be eliminated in favour of the crest (*Luck* and *Casino*). In terms of similarity, it can be said that *Luck* and *Chance* on the one hand, and *Chance* and *Casino* on the other, are closer to each other than *Luck* and *Casino*.

On the basis of the maximum tree, one can answer the question asked by Abric and Vacherot about the identification of the words associated with game or problem solving as a representation of the task. Flament (1986, 144) proposed the following reading:

> Let us eliminate from the maximum tree the crests found
> between items of different initial categories (see Figure). The sub-
> graphs thus obtained are then homogeneous in their composition

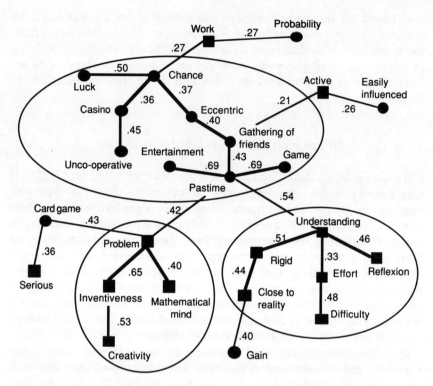

Figure 1.9 *Graphic representation of the maximum tree of the similarity system of the representation of a task.*

Note: The items classified *a priori* as 'game' are represented by a full circle and those classified *a priori* as 'problem-solving' by a square. The crests in bold type link items of same categories together. The similarity indices are noted along the crests. According to Flament, 1986, 142.

(either all game or all problem solving). One observes isolated items (such as *work*, *probability* and *active*) whose initial meaning is seriously called into question (since each of them is more similar to items of the opposite category than to the items of its own category). There remain three major subgraphs [shown in Figure 1.9] – one for game and two for problem solving – whose items see their initial meaning confirmed in the representation by the proximity of items of the same category.

One will find other applications of this method to illustrate, for instance, the structure of the field of representation of pupils by their teachers (Gilly, 1972) or the transformation of a SR (that of hunting by hunters) or, more specifically, the reorganization of its elements (Guimelli, 1989).

2

Automatic Cluster Analysis and Multidimensional Scaling

The structures revealed by HCA must, of course, be read according to the entered data. As shown above, these data may derive from quite different questionings. We also wish to make it clear that this is an item classification established according to a proximity criterion. As shown in the other chapters, one cannot assert that the representational field thus highlighted is necessarily common to the individuals or groups that compose the study population.

The above-discussed classification techniques aim to elucidate the manner in which the elements of a SR are categorized. The criterion used for classification depends on the proximity or similarity of the elements. The use of such an analysis therefore ensues from the (often implicit) assumption that subjects respond by comparing the elements and classifying them. One also assumes that subjects or groups of subjects share the same category referent and that there are consensual views of the classification of the SR field elements. HCA reveals an order in the inter-element links but shows the heterogeneity of categories. When this heterogeneity increases, the postulate underlying the analysis weakens, and the results become vague.

In fact, rather than categorizing the field elements, subjects may distinguish between degrees. One must then consider that field organization is not, or is not limited to, classification (between what applies and what does not apply to such a definition or between what describes such-and-such an aspect, for example), but is based on the positioning of the elements on one or more dimensions (degree of application of such a definition or degree of description of such-and-such an aspect). We will now consider two data-analysis methods that enable us to apprehend field organization by reducing the field elements to dimensions of which they are reference points.

These techniques are often used in a more ambitious perspective as part of the study of objectification. Using multivariate analyses such as multidimensional scaling (MDS) or correspondence factor analysis (CFA), a number of authors intend to define more complex structures by sometimes involving various dimensions and thus extracting a more central structure compared with other possible modulations. The postulate inherent in this position is that data organization in a multidimensional space resulting from these analyses would, in a way, express the cognitive organization of the SR's field elements. The cognitive structure is thus assumed to be more complex than the one postulating a 'simple' classification of the elements. Subjects would not share (or share not only) a common category referent but (also) information-processing functions involving different criteria of cutoff, organization and orientation of the field elements.

Multidimensional Scaling: Common Structure of Social Representations

MDS techniques (see Beauvois, Roulin and Tiberghien, 1990, 202-4, for introduction to this analytic technique) are based, like HCA, on interstimulus proximity coefficients. MDS enables different stimuli to be placed on a limited number of dimensions (usually two or three) by preserving the relations of distance between them. The number of dimensions chosen depends on the fit of the model (represented distances) for basic data (observed dissimilarities). The model fit is indicated by a 'stress' measurement which gives the percentage of empirical dissimilarities that are inconsistent with the represented distances. When there is a perfect ascending relationship between the two measurements, i.e., when the distances resulting from MDS and the observed dissimilarities are arranged identically, the stress equals zero. It is generally admitted that a stress below 0.10 allows the model fit to be considered satisfactory (cf. Kruskal's presentation, 1964). As previously, MDS will deal with an inter-stimulus proximity matrix. The results are usually interpreted by reading the graph on which the stimulus co-ordinates are projected on two dimensions. To interpret the dimensions, one can perform correlations between the co-ordinates of the multidimensionally scaled elements with assessments or evaluations of these same elements.

Multidimensional Scaling of Word Associations

According to some authors, a comparison of dictionaries enables them to conclude that there is a specific structure of a SR. In this case, the similarity matrix is often treated by MDS. Sometimes, MDS follows HCA to define the groups of stimuli created by the latter more closely. To show the difference between the field organization resulting from HCA and MDS, we will revert to Di Giacomo's illustration described above.

Illustration: a Protest Movement

Di Giacomo (1980) used MDS to clarify the results obtained by HCA. With three dimensions, MDS is well suited for the observed dissimilarity matrix (stress = 0.02). The first dimension opposes political extremism (of both right and left) to *workers* and, to a lesser extent, to *executives, students* and *AGL*. This dimension bears out the confusion over the two political extremisms and their separation from the other universes obtained by HCA. In fact, the spreading out of words on this dimension seems to show that the words common to dictionaries make it possible not so much to categorize the stimulus words as to place them in different places of a scale expressing the level of political commitment.

The second dimension separates the *committee* against the 10 000 (*strike, power* and *workers* being on the same side of the axis) from *students* – a word close to *executives* and *extreme right*. This dimension makes clearer the distinction between the universe associated with *students* and that associated with the *committee*. The third dimension opposes *AGL* to *power*, since the words *extreme right* and *executives* are the only ones to be found on the same side of the axis as *power*. The author showed that this axis can be interpreted as a distinction between those who have *power* and those who have no *power* on the one hand, and between what is protest-related and what is institutional on the other. The fabric of oppositions revealed by MDS enables us to answer more firmly the question asked by the author about the *committee*'s failure. The *committee*'s strategy and political leanings are clearly distinguished from the *student* universe. The latter is associated not only with passive protest against the institutionalized *power* but also with elements that characterize it as *executives*. In Di Giacomo's view, the *committee* seemed like an outgroup to *students* (at least when he conducted his research), and they were thus unable to commit themselves to the *committee*-led movement.

MDS yields results that are easier to interpret than those obtained by HCA. One may wonder if MDS clarifies the groupings obtained by HCA, or if it proposes a more suitable and self-sufficient data organization grid, or if the three large groups composing the hierarchical tree do not better represent the relationship which students establish between different stimulus words. It is difficult to choose among these options. It seems, however, that the semantic proximities between dictionaries depend more on a distinction between different dimensions on which each stimulus word indicates a degree (of political connotation, student preoccupation and protest against power) than on a clear categorization of these three aspects. To support this conclusion, let us recall that the coefficients of similarity between dictionaries were low. Moreover, accounting for such a limited number of data by means of a three-dimensional space leads us to think that, in this specific case, the results obtained by MDS are unstable.

Illustration: Mental Illness

We will take another example of the use of MDS from De Rosa (1987, 1988), who conducted a study on mental illness – one of a host of studies carried out on this theme in Italy. Di Giacomo (1987, 68–9) summarized as follows the principal components of the structure of SRs which these studies revealed:

> Roughly speaking, this structure is based on three poles: (1) definition of the normal person, (2) definition of the mad person and (3) definition of the ill person
>
> This is inferred from the fact that, in all the cases that I have examined, the factor space is determined by these three stimuli. Each time, in fact, the first two factors are the product of the NORMAL-versus-MORBIDITY opposition, on the one hand, and of the MAD-versus-ILL opposition on the other. This observation might appear banal and fairly obvious to some people. Nothing of the kind! Specific contents demonstrate it. These contents show remarkable dualism. Let us first consider the contents associated with the NORMAL PERSON. This person is described as balanced and healthy, calm, sure of him-/herself, consistent and rational, active and hard-working, serene, sociable and communicative, happy, content and satisfied.
>
> As in echo, versus this utopian personality, we find the morbidity described in terms of the MAD PERSON and the ILL PERSON. The former is characterized by strangeness, originality and restlessness. This person is represented as irrational and unpredictable with strong emotional reactions. Marginalized, he/she is inactive, alone and desperate. As for the latter, our sample subjects attribute primarily suffering, weakness, neediness and dependence to this person. Professionals provide assistance to such persons and show understanding for these traits.
>
> What we are witnessing here is therefore a curious (though expected) echo phenomenon that dichotomizes human experience. Happiness is the fruit of normality (though admittedly banal), whereas irrationality, unpredictability and inactivity

(even restless one) cause suffering and isolation. Thus, the most banal and common human experience is excluded from normality, explained away in social terms and managed in medical terms.

De Rosa's research involved 1884 subjects from three contrasting regions of Italy belonging to different social categories (such as children/adults and professionals/non-professionals). Unlike Di Giacomo's research on a student protest movement, we have here a heterogeneous population. The author used five stimulus words: *normal, mad, mentally ill, ill* and *oneself*. A similarity matrix was built for each specific category of subjects. The matrix was then treated by MDS.

The author thus obtained as many graphic spaces as different groups (e.g., samples from Rome, rural regions, students and professionals) which she compared. Let us mention, by way of example, the bidimensional space obtained by MDS on the sample from Rome, since the spaces resulting from the other samples (samples from rural regions, students and professionals) were comparable to it.

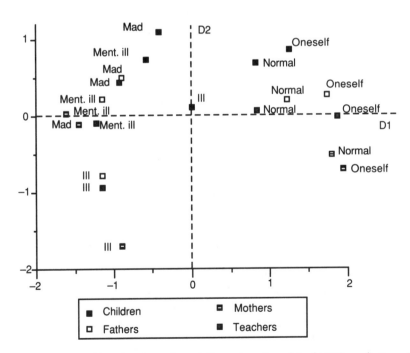

Figure 2.1 *Graphic representation of dimensions 1 and 2 of MDS on dictionaries of words associated with the stimulus words used by De Rosa in her study of SRs of mental illness.*

Note: Stress equals 0.117. Figure adapted from De Rosa, 1988.

> De Rosa found that the bidimensional space obtained by Kruskal's
> MDS method from the matrices of similarity between stimulus
> words revealed a structure that is found in all groups [. . .] The
> structural configuration, which emerges in both children and
> adults from various regions (Bologna, Rome, Naples and rural
> areas) without major differences in sex, social class (for all groups)
> and age (for children), clearly opposes, on the horizontal axis, the
> sphere of 'normality' (*normal person* and *self*) to that of abnormality
> (*ill, mentally ill* and *mad*). On the other axis, the area of physical
> pathology (*ill*) is the opposite of that of mental deviance (*mentally
> ill* and *mad*). (1988, 35)

The above two illustrations are based on a consensual view of SRs.
Admittedly, De Rosa showed that one and the same dimensional space
enabled her to account for the contrasts between different stimulus targets given by different groups of subjects. It is none the less a fact that
treating the semantic material maximizes the homogeneity of these contrasts. The semantic variety between individuals or groups of individuals is erased, which fortunately simplifies field organization on the one
hand and reduces its meaning on the other.

The research which we will now discuss was designed to illustrate the
complexity and difficulty of using MDS to treat more heterogeneous
material. We will verify the methodological and interpretative enrich-
ment this research provided.

Multidimensional Scaling of Heterogeneous Data

Illustration: Implicit Theories of Personality

Works on implicit theories of personality (cf. Nisbett and Ross, 1980;
Leyens, 1983; Beauvois, 1982, 1984; Paicheler, 1984; Semin, 1987) can be
easily approached from the angle of the study of SRs and particularly of
objectification. These works deal, in fact, with the cognitive systems that
organize relations between personality traits. During its initial development, research on the implicit theories of personality (ITP) focused on
permanent and universal logics that would guide the inference of psychological attributes from a trait or a behaviour. Another approach has
gradually invested this concept by placing it in the area of perception of
others and of impression formation and by drawing it more towards
that of representation (Aldrovanti, Beauvois and Guingouin, 1987, 117).

Their link with the study of SRs is all the closer as the ITP are related
to certain scientific production, i.e. that of test psychology, leading to a
theory of personality. One is thus in a position to refer to exchanges or

communication between scientific and popular discourses. Paicheler (1984, 295) defined the connection between ITP and SRs as follows:

> The causality schemata, defined individually and functioning 'in the head' of each specific individual, reflect primarily a social causality and the way different groups conceive and explain, through their perception, the evolution of social life, the conflicts and the hierarchical systems that characterize it. The efficacy of the process lies in the fact that, while subjects do not 'know' the theory, they use it and are used by it. If they are capable of stating its effects, its logic would elude them [. . .] Through SRs, we are dealing with objects and not with concepts. While, as shown by Moscovici in connection with the spread of psychoanalysis, these notions of common sense were initially concepts within a certain framework of scientific theory, they are now reobjectified. This latter process is also accompanied by a schematization and the construction of an implicit theory that has no longer anything to do with the initial theory.

We will not discuss here different conceptions of the ITP, whether they appear as the spread of scientific knowledge or, on the contrary, as the objectified foundation of this knowledge. We will simply illustrate the studies conducted in this area often using multivariate techniques such as MDS. This technique is employed to reveal the structure of traits that are most commonly used to describe others.

We will now look at a study conducted by Rosenberg and Sedlack (1972). The authors asked 100 subjects to describe ten persons: five well known to them and five known to them by repute. Subjects were told that at least five adjectives or short phrases were needed to make these different descriptions. From the responses thus obtained, the authors extracted 7057 semantic units which they reduced to categories of traits by aggregating the units with the same basic morpheme (example: 'sincere person', 'fairly sincere' and 'always sincere' are classified under the trait 'sincere'). Finally, they chose 110 traits cited at least ten times to describe one of the stimulus persons of whom eighty were selected for MDS (the program used did not allow more than eighty items to be entered!). The measure calculated by the authors was based on the frequency of co-occurrences of each pair of traits weighted by the number of times the same subject used the same descriptor to characterize several persons.

The dimensionality of the space required for achieving an acceptable fit to data was high: with five dimensions, the stress was about 0.15. Rosenberg and Sedlack (1972) attributed this result to the fact that free associations would be a less stable measure of inter-item associations than the presentation of a closed list of traits and/or that the (more

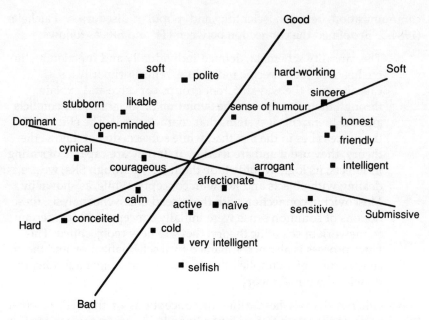

Figure 2.2   *Graphic representation of dimensions 1 and 2 of MDS on the personality traits associated freely with different individuals*

Note: The straight line of regression of opinions on three scales of different traits were entered into this figure. Figure adapted from Rosenberg and Sedlack, 1972, 158.

numerous) traits resulting from free associations would refer to a dimensionality more complex than that corresponding to the traits of a closed list (see the study by Rosenberg, Nelson and Vivekananthan, 1968). To reduce the number of dimensions while keeping a stress acceptable, the authors subjected the matrices of intermediate distances obtained by the first MDS to a second MDS. The reader interested in this procedure is referred to the original text. Finally, the authors proposed a bidimensional configuration (see Rosenberg and Sedlack, 1972, 158), of which we will give a general idea.

To interpret the multidimensional space, the authors also asked other subjects to rate the selected traits on nine bipolar scales chosen from previous research (Rosenberg and Olshan, 1970) and on nine scales corresponding to the classic dimensions of Osgood's semantic differential, i.e. the dimensions of evaluation, potency and activity (Osgood, Suci and Tannenbaum, 1957). It was then possible to calculate correlations between the rating of traits on each scale and the two dimensions and to trace on the bidimensional space the axes corresponding to the best correlated axes. This procedure will be discussed in more detail later.

The authors interpreted the space of traits as follows. They first observed that the perception of personality was strongly structured by evaluation. They noticed, in fact, that the evaluative scales *good/bad* and *social success/failure* were closely correlated with each dimension. This was also the case, but at a lower level, for the scale *intellectual success*. This latter result seemed surprising because *intelligent* was the trait most frequently cited by subjects. In the authors' view, this point was probably due to the fact that subjects rarely described others as stupid. Another axis that appeared clearly in the space was associated with the dimension *hard/soft*. The authors found, however, that this axis was far from being orthogonal to that of evaluation, which is usually found in studies using the semantic differential. Finally, the authors noted that the space was difficult to interpret fully (unlike the one obtained by a closed-questioning technique). For one thing, a pluridimensional space would have to be considered and, for another, the orientation given to the space, other than evaluation, was based on the axis *dominant/submissive* – an orientation difficult to understand, to say the least. In fact, traits such as *soft* and *open-minded* were found near the dominant pole of the axis, while a trait such as *arrogant* was found at the submissive pole of the axis.

It is interesting to note, as did Rosenberg, Nelson and Vivekananthan, that the dimensional space built from data collected by closed questioning is less complex and easier to interpret than the one worked out from data gathered by open questioning. In other words, it is easier to find (at least by a procedure such as MDS) a simple structural organization when one controls *a priori* the stimuli (on which subjects express their opinion) than when these stimuli are generated by subjects themselves.

We conclude our description of MDS with the above illustration of the use of this method in the treatment of heterogeneous data. It should be noted in passing that works on the ITP are based sometimes on highly complex multivariate analysis techniques (see, for example, Gärlin, 1976; Semin and Chassein, 1985, and Rosenberg's 1988 work on social personality and autobiography). This example shows, in fact, the difficulty that may be encountered in taking into account the variety of individual responses (of free-association type) for extracting a simple and readable structure of it. Undoubtedly, a number of inter-individual or inter-stimulus variations sometimes prevent us from accounting for a single representational field.

Before reverting to the meaning of the dimensional space, we will deal with correspondence factor analysis, which is based on another technique of treating distances but raises the same problem as MDS as far as the interpretation of results is concerned.

3

Correspondence Factor Analysis:

Mapping of Structuring Elements

Correspondence factor analysis (CFA) is better known to French-speaking researchers than MDS. No wonder, therefore, that CFA is more often used in the study of SRs than other multivariate analysis techniques.

CFA is a technique for treating various types of data matrices such as contingency and frequency tables. It is based on the hypothesis that the table's rows and columns are independent of each other. Treatment is based on the breakup of the table or the basic matrix into different simpler tables that enable us to account for deviations from independence expressed by the Chi-square method. CFA reclassifies the rows and columns so as to arrange those that match and then ranks each of them. This procedure makes it possible to maximize the association between the two systems (rows and columns) – an association whose closeness is indicated by a correlation coefficient (the eigenvalue of a dimension is interpreted as Pearson's r, the R^2 or 'lambda'). This procedure also makes it possible to determine the position of each of the rows and columns (or more simply of the modalities) on the factor (or the dimension). Generally, a single dimension does not enable us to account for the deviations from independence contained in one and the same matrix. CFA searches for a second dimension by the same procedure, but by seeking a degree of maximum association that is independent of the first and so on. The results can be interpreted by using the graphs on which the co-ordinates of the rows and columns appear on two dimensions. To make it easier to read the figure (and avoid certain traps inherent in the objectification of spatial representations), CFA provides the relative contribution of the factor to each modality (i.e., at which point the factor accounts for the variation in this modality) and the absolute contribution (i.e., the contribution of each modality to the amount of variance explained by the factor). This latter information enables the dimensions to be interpreted and named (for a more detailed and easily accessible description, see

44

Lorenzi-Cioldi, 1983; Cibois, 1983; Beauvois, Roulin and Tiberghien, 1990).

We will give two examples of the use of CFA. The first will illustrate a classic way of treating a contingency table, while the second will concern a common but somewhat special use of CFA.

Illustration: Attraction and Rejection of Occupations

This first example is taken from a survey conducted among apprentices on the SRs of work. They were asked to check off three occupations they liked best and three others they liked least on a list of fourteen occupations hardly accessible or inaccessible to these apprentices because of the training or financial investment they required or because they did not exist in the region from which the subjects came. Let us emphasize that there are a host of works on the SRs of occupations or of work (see, for example, Burton, 1972; De Polo and Sarchielli, 1983; Huteau, 1976; Lorenzi-Cioldi and Joye, 1988; Salmaso and Pombeni, 1986). The present example should be considered a limited illustration of this research area.

We will first give the percentage of subjects who classified each of these occupations among those they liked best or least (see Table 3.1).

One finds that the occupations most appreciated by the subjects were, on the one hand, those that, despite everything, seemed to them the

Table 3.1 *Attraction and rejection of occupations by apprentices*

Occupations	They like best	They like least
Racing driver	50	9
Photographer	43	5
Journalist	33	8
Engineer	21	9
Actor	28	20
Chemist	19	13
Farmer	27	24
Social worker	17	14
Doctor	9	15
Teacher	13	22
Banker	12	21
Lawyer	8	31
Psychologist	8	35
Coal miner	2	54

Note: The above table shows the percentage of subjects who declared that they liked or did not like such-and-such an occupation. The occupations are listed in order of preference (difference between attraction and rejection). The respondents numbered 340.

most accessible (such as engineer and farmer) and, on the other, those that, glorified by the media, fuelled wild career plans: racing driver, photographer, journalist and actor. Conversely, liberal professions, albeit enjoying considerable social prestige, and those in the area of educational psychology, perhaps because of their female connotation, were not highly prized. Liberal professions also require a training which the subjects were unable to receive. On the other hand, the occupation of coal miner, rejected by nearly everyone, was not only virtually absent in the universe of these apprentices but also had a number of serious drawbacks such as hard working conditions and the difficulty of getting out of them.

We selected two modalities for each of the fourteen occupations: (1) classifying it among those liked best (acceptance) and (2) classifying it among those liked least (rejection). A sample population of ninety subjects was chosen randomly from among the 340 respondents. We thus obtained a rectangular matrix composed of ninety rows (subjects) and twenty-eight columns (acceptance and rejection of fourteen occupations) containing codes 0 or 1, depending on whether the modality was absent or present. This matrix was subjected to a CFA.

Let us look first at the quality of the factors obtained by CFA. Table 3.2 below indicates the eigenvalues of the first nine factors, the percentages of explained variance and a histogram of the eigenvalues.

Factor 1 has a high eigenvalue for this type of data. Let us recall that the square root of the eigenvalue indicates the coefficient of correlation between rows and columns for which the factor accounts. In our case, it is higher than 0.40. The histogram shows that from factor 5 on, the eigenvalues remain more or less unchanged, which is generally considered an

Table 3.2 *Level of the first nine factors of CFA on the attraction and rejection of occupations*

Factor	Eigen-value	% expl.	% cumul.	Histogram of eigenvalues
1	0.164	21.98	21.98	*****************************
2	0.088	11.80	33.79	****************
3	0.078	10.56	44.35	**************
4	0.064	8.64	53.00	************
5	0.051	6.83	59.84	*********
6	0.042	5.71	65.55	********
7	0.042	5.63	71.19	********
8	0.032	4.32	75.51	******
9	0.030	4.07	79.58	******

indication for keeping the number of factors below this threshold.

We will first examine the first three factors that account for 44.4 per cent of variance. This percentage is appreciable, but it must be borne in mind that there remains a high percentage of data variation to be explained. Table 3.3 provides, by way of example, information that helps interpret the CFA results for two modalities.

Table 3.3 shows the weight (WEIGHT) of each modality, i.e., the frequency with which each modality is cited, the inertia of each of the modalities (INR), i.e., the total contribution of each modality to the deviation from independence: the number represents a percentage (total = 1000) that is all the higher as the modality deviates from independence and thereby helps orient the axes. Table 3.3 also shows the elements that enable each modality to be located on the different factors: the co-ordinates (Co-ord), the relative contributions (RCO: part of the modality for which the factor accounts) and the absolute contributions (CTR: the modality's contribution to the composition of the factor). This latter information is used to specify the factors on the basis of the modalities whose CTR is the largest (for instance, larger than the mean, the total of the CTR being equal to 1000. In Figure 3.1, we indicate in bold type and italics the contributions exceeding 36, i.e. 1000/number of modalities, on each factor).

To interpret different factors, we will use graphs on to which the co-ordinates of the different modalities of two axes are projected.

The first axis opposes the occupations *racing driver* and *farmer* to the professions *banker, lawyer* and *psychologist*, while the second axis opposes the professions *engineer, teacher* and *banker* to the professions *lawyer* and *psychologist*. Moreover, one notices on this axis that the attraction of these latter professions, located on the negative pole of the axis, goes hand in hand with the rejection not only of the occupations located on the positive pole of the axis but also of *photographer*, whereas *racing driver* and *social worker* are negatively associated with the occupations located on the positive pole. Let us also note that the relative contributions (RCO) indicate that these two axes account for one-third to half of the variations in the modalities that orient these factors most.

In summary, the first two factors allow three separate groups of occupations (on one and/or the other axis) to emerge: two occupations (*racing driver* and *farmer*) that are among those preferred by the apprentices, two generally unattractive professions (*lawyer* and *psychologist*) and three fairly appreciated professions (*banker, engineer* and *teacher*). The significance of the inter-occupational associations that thus emerge is that they depend not only on the degree of their attractiveness or unattractiveness. CFA shows that subjects tend to classify (among the occupations they like best or least) each group of above-mentioned occupations together. Moreover, one observes that preference for one of

Table 3.3 Description of the first three factors of CFA on attraction and rejection: weights, co-ordinates and contributions of modalities

Mod.	WEIGHT	INR	Factor 1 Co-ord	1 RCO	1 CTR	2 Co-ord	2 RCO	2 CTR	3 Coord	3 RCO	3 CTR
act+	65	22	225	204	20	-24	2	0	48	9	2
ban+	14	51	-1185	503	116	524	98	42	-285	29	14
che+	36	37	-272	96	16	293	111	35	-168	36	13
doc+	14	40	-329	49	9	-458	95	32	258	30	11
dri+	86	21	267	394	37	33	6	1	-83	38	7
eng+	42	30	-177	59	8	348	228	58	95	17	5
far+	39	35	527	413	66	-106	17	5	-169	42	14
jou+	43	31	159	47	7	-127	30	8	145	39	11
law+	16	49	-1020	444	98	-664	188	77	-365	57	26
min+	2	49	1220	78	18	-144	1	0	-3522	654	305
pho+	80	18	248	354	30	-35	7	1	68	27	5
psy+	16	50	-1021	431	98	-863	308	131	-159	10	5
soc+	35	31	-193	56	8	9	0	0	355	191	55
tea+	17	40	-491	140	26	484	136	46	357	74	28
act-	25	37	-255	59	10	-2	0	0	29	1	0
ban-	35	34	61	5	1	-628	539	157	171	40	13
che-	27	34	408	179	28	-62	4	1	296	94	30
doc-	27	33	320	114	17	113	14	4	202	45	14
dri-	16	55	-1193	575	143	507	104	48	-122	6	3
eng-	14	44	653	177	35	-680	191	71	-641	170	71
far-	44	32	-412	307	45	-103	19	5	53	5	2
jou-	17	42	83	4	1	300	50	18	-1048	604	243
law-	58	23	194	126	13	109	39	8	149	74	16
min-	103	13	-118	150	9	162	281	31	57	35	4
pho-	6	54	-1842	485	120	-878	110	51	-469	31	16
psy-	63	23	165	102	11	175	115	22	55	11	2
soc-	28	38	219	47	8	339	114	37	-477	225	81
tea-	31	33	133	22	3	-558	396	109	71	6	2

Note: See the text for reading this table.

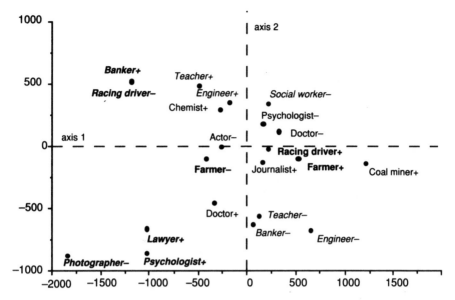

Figure 3.1 *Graphic representation of modalities on the first two factor axes of CFA on the attraction and rejection of fourteen occupations.*

Note: CFA involves ninety individuals and twenty-eight modalities. The modalities in bold type have the largest contributions on the first factor and those in italics on the second factor. A + sign indicates that the occupation is chosen, while a – sign indicates that it is rejected. Part of the modalities contributing little to the orientation of the two axes are not named.

the groups of occupations is often linked to the rejection of the other groups. This is especially true of the opposition between *engineer, teacher* and *banker* on the one hand, and *lawyer* and *psychologist* on the other, since these two professional groups are also distinct from *racing driver* and *farmer*. While it is easy to account for the opposition revealed by the first axis (liberal professions considered unattractive versus occupations generally found attractive by the apprentices), it is more difficult to interpret the distinction made by the second axis. In all likelihood, one can account for this response structure only by identifying the characteristics of the subjects who generate it. We will revert to similar problems when dealing with anchoring in social groups (Part Three).

Reading the graph will show that the modalities farthest from the axis centre are not necessarily those that help orient the axis most (this is particularly true of *coal miner* when this occupation is chosen). This point leads us to emphasize a risk of CFA: its homothetic effect. CFA reveals the structure of deviations from independence but not their degree. Thus, by reading only the graphs, one may be led to 'make learned comments on a table where the deviations from independence are so minimal that they might just as well be due to chance' (Cibois, 1983, 123). Hence the need to consider also eigenvalues and other indications (contributions) provided by CFA.

An examination of the third factor can be brief. The contribution of a single occupation is larger than the mean of the positive side of the axis (that of *social worker* classified as attractive). *Journalist, engineer* and *social worker*, when rejected, appear on the negative pole of the axis along with *coal miner* classified as attractive. This factor provides hardly any information in addition to locating *social worker* and *coal miner* better, the former close to the relatively well accepted professions such as *journalist* and *engineer* and the latter flatly rejected in a broadly consensual manner. It may none the less be said that the preference given to professions such as *journalist, social worker* or *engineer* goes hand in hand with the flat rejection of *coal miner*. Once again, this opposition probably acquires a meaning by referring to the groups of subjects who generate it.

The structure that emerges from these findings is fairly special compared with the above-mentioned works that focused on the study of occupations (see also Part Two). In these works, there generally appeared a first axis oriented by social status or prestige associated with occupations. In our case, perhaps because the question put to subjects implied a value judgement, which should not, *a priori*, weaken field organization based on professional prestige, we call special attention to axes less easy to name but whose consistency can none the less be apprehended through the classification logics that can be partly inferred from the extent to which the occupations are accepted or rejected. Let us be cautious, however, and recall that the above-discussed factors accounted for only part of the dispersion of responses and especially that the key to interpretation may lie more in the characteristics of subjects who classify than in the classification itself. This example shows the limits of an approach to SRs confined to the study of objectification.

Correspondence Analysis of Words

Illustration: Representation of Participation

Le Bouedec's research (1984) on SRs of participation encouraged several researchers to use a similar methodology (see, for example, Monteil and Mailhot, 1988, on training or Galli and Nigro, 1986, on power). The author wanted to 'show how one can study quantitatively each component' of SRs, more particularly the field and its attitudinal orientation (Le Bouedec, 1984, 247).

The author first asked a first sample population of 128 subjects to associate thirty nouns with the concept 'participation' and then gave them twenty adjectives likely to describe this concept best. From this material, the author selected the twenty-six most common nouns to which he added the stimulus word to submit them to a paired comparison (cf. Costermans, 1979). Each subject was asked to indicate on a five-point scale the degree of similarity between each pair of words. This was assuredly a long and tedious task (351 pairs of words to be rated) that discouraged a number of subjects (only 348 out of 600 protocols were judged complete).

As the concepts were compared on a five-point similarity scale, five matrices (which showed the percentages of subjects who considered that two concepts were similar to a certain degree) were built, i.e. one matrix per degree of similarity. Only the matrix corresponding to the highest degree of similarity was subjected to a CFA (the author noted that this matrix was most useful for showing factors). Le Bouedec discussed the first three factors that accounted for 70.8 per cent of variance. The first factor, which accounted for 44.8 per cent of variance all by itself, was directed to a pole by the words *profit*, *interest* and *employer* and to the other pole by the words *friendship*, *dialogue*, *joy*, *sharing* and *understanding*. This factor was considered to express 'an axiological dimension of participation' (Le Bouedec, 1984, 259), i.e., a dimension centring on the values that were negative on the one hand and positive on the other. However, it is difficult to follow the author's suggestion that one of the poles would denote 'good' participation and the other 'bad' participation. The words associated with participation, such as *interest* or *employer*, and thus the dimension with which they are associated, may very well be considered antonyms, i.e. opposites of participation. Was this not, moreover, what Le Bouedec meant when he ended the discussion of this first factor by suggesting that 'the original fund of participation refers mostly to the idea of fusional relations' (ibid., 259)?

The second factor (16.2 per cent of variance) was directed, on the one hand, by the 'values' located on the first axis (*profit*, *understanding*, *interest*, *joy*, *friendship* and *employer*) and, on the other, by the words evoking the organization of social relationships (*worker*, *work*, *society*, *labour union* and *politics*). The author interpreted this axis as the individual-versus-collective opposition coupled with the opposition between a conservative view and a progressive view of participation. Finally, the third factor (9.8 per cent of variance) denoted a distinction between words associated rather with specific action (*worker*, *help* and *work*) and others associated more with discourse (*student*, *expression*, *discussion* and *meeting*). Let us also note that this axis opposed the worker's universe to the student's universe.

In the light of these three factors, the representational field of participation appeared structured, according to Le Bouedec, around the fol-

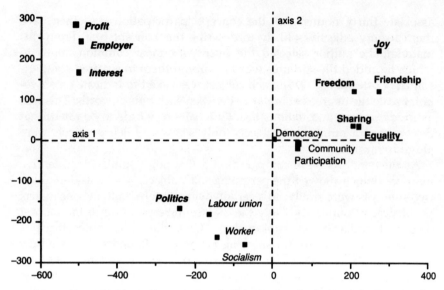

Figure 3.2 *Graphic representation of modalities on the first two factor axes of CFA on similarity between the words usually associated with participation*

Note: The modalities in bold type have the largest contributions on the first factor and those in italics on the second factor. Part of the modalities contributing little to the orientation of the two axes are not named. According to Le Bouedec, 1984, 200.

lowing three major axes: (1) an axis centring on exchange relationship, friendship and sharing, (2) an axis centring on individual achievements and interpersonal harmony and (3) an axis centring on expression and discussion.

This interpretation was based on the inertia of modalities, i.e., on their distance from the centre of gravity. The author considered, in fact, that the closer the modality was to the centre of gravity, the better it defined the field, because it was then closer to the stimulus word. This interpretation is debatable. The modalities close to the centre of gravity are those that scarcely deviate from the hypothesis of independence, i.e., those whose frequency of similarities to the other words hardly varies. From the inertia criterion, therefore, one cannot conclude that these words better define, or are closer to, participation. Such a conclusion can be drawn only from the degree of similarity between these words and participation.

The word *participation* as well as words such as *community, responsibility* and *democracy* provide an absolute contribution to the first three factors that are negligible. One therefore concludes that their proximity to the words that help orient these factors is comparable. In other words, the universe of abstract and personal values (such as *joy*, *friendship* and *freedom*) and that of employers, which oppose each other on the first factor, organize the representation of the semantic field suitable for the representation of participation. It seems, therefore, more correct to say that the field of participation is structured first by this opposition which is corrected by the second factor on which the universe associated with workers – a universe distinguishable from the two poles organizing the first axis – is located. Finally, the student-centred universe appearing on the third factor in opposition to the workers' universe modulates and supplements the structure.

Le Bouedec used attitude scales to analyze the field's attitudinal orientation. Describing this point will enable us to deal with the last chapter of this part on the field's attitudinal component.

4

Interpretation of the Dimensions of a Social Representational Field

The third component of the SR field is the attitude towards the object. The general question to be answered is how to determine the field's evaluative connotation. More specifically, one aims to interpret the dimensional space (of both MDS and CFA) by comparing the position of the elements on the dimensions with the opinion given by individuals on them on different scales. It is then possible to name one or more orientations of the field and to give a direction to the dimensions. MDS and CFA enable us to describe data organization by reducing data to a few major axes which we try to name. By superposing on to this description opinions that are independent of the structure revealed by multivariate analysis, one seeks to interpret it by seeing if the field elements are arranged according to their evaluative connotation. The results of this operation may lead us to conclusions stressing the importance of latent variables (cognitive systems and/or social gravities) in the objectification of such-and-such a concept.

Attitude Scales and Metastructure

A number of studies dealt with this aspect using Osgood's semantic differential (Osgood, Suci and Tannenbaum, 1957). Usually, this tool is not used in its classic form but is modified and adapted to the object of SRs. Let us recall that the semantic differential is designed to measure, on a battery of bipolar scales, the affective level of subjects' relationship with any object. Responses to the different scales of the semantic differential are often correlated, and it appears that three dimensions (evaluation, potency and activity) enable us to account for the variation in responses. Certain scales correspond closely with these three dimensions, for example: *good–bad* for the evaluation dimension, *strong–weak* for the potency dimension and *fast–slow* for the activity dimension (cf. Heise, 1970). This three-dimensional structure was hotly debated. Thus, one pondered the independence of these dimensions and the amount of variance explained by each of them (see, for example, Summers, 1970). One wonders if this structure is not, after all, the cognitive framework of all objectification – a metastructure governing the organization of any representational field? This debate goes far beyond the bounds of our problem, and we will deal with it only incidentally.

We will look especially into the use of the semantic differential in the studies of SRs.

Illustration: 'Good' Participation

In his above-discussed research, Le Bouedec also asked his subjects to rate the twenty-seven concepts chosen for paired comparison on seventeen bipolar scales. Nine were taken from Osgood's semantic differential, three per dimension: *good–bad, kind–unkind* and *pleasant–unpleasant* for the evaluation dimension; *strong–weak, big–small* and *huge–tiny* for the potency dimension; and *lively–indolent, slow–fast* and *old–young* for the activity dimension. From the adjectives most frequently associated with participation, the author built eight other bipolar scales: *open–closed, easy–difficult, useful–useless, possible–impossible, false–true, effective–ineffective, active–passive* and *familiar–unfamiliar*.

The author analyzed the attitudinal orientation of the SRs of participation by subjecting to a CFA a matrix composed of the twenty-seven concepts (twenty-six words most frequently associated with participation plus this word itself) and the seventeen scales. The first three factors thus obtained accounted for 45.2 per cent, 13.6 per cent and 6.9 per cent of variance respectively. Projecting the concepts on to different axes prompted the author to consider that the factors thus obtained were comparable to those obtained by CFA based on similarity between words. Le Bouedec formed two groups of scales from the percentage of variance which they explained and their absolute contribution to the factors. It thus became apparent that the scales *pleasant–unpleasant, good–bad, kind–unkind, true–false* and *open–closed* strongly oriented the first factor, while the scales *young–old* and *big–small* provided a considerable contribution to the second factor. The direction of the first factor was provided by the opposition between words denoting 'individual' or 'inter-individual' values (such as *job, friendship, freedom, help* and *understanding*) and words denoting more 'social' aspects (such as *society, employer, politics* and *socialism*). The four scales that contributed most to this factor ranged from their positive pole (*pleasant, good, kind* and *true*) to their negative pole (*unpleasant, bad, unkind* and *false*) from the first to the second side of the axis. The evaluation dimension clearly defined the first factor.

The second axis opposed the words contributing most to the first factor to more 'concrete' entities (such as *student, worker, group* and *meeting*). It is interesting to note that the second factor (much weaker than the first) was a good illustration of the correctness of the approximation of the data provided by the first factor. Two scales dependent on the potency dimension helped orient the second axis. The 'strong' pole (*big* or *huge*) was close to the words defining the first factor (such as *society, employer, friendship, joy* and *politics*), while the 'weak' pole (*small* or *tiny*) was associated with the opposite words (such as *student, worker, group* and *meeting*). Moreover, the scale *young–old* (activity dimension) ranged from its 'active' pole to its 'passive' pole in the direction opposite to the potency dimension. It should be noted that, unlike the evaluation dimension, the potency and activity dimensions had little weight in the orientation of the axes. This result may be interpreted by the fact that 'participation would not be experienced as a very dynamic reality' (Le Bouedec, 1984, 268). It should be noted, however, that a number of studies have emphasized that the evaluative factor accounted for a much larger percentage of the variation in responses to the semantic differential than did the other two factors.

To conclude our chapter on the orientation of the SRs of participation, we may quote Le Bouedec (ibid., 267):

> As far as participation is perceived as a reality freed from economic, social and political constraints (all constraints are perceived as rather or fairly unpleasant) and expressing, on the contrary, a sort of more or less discarnate transparency, then, and to this extent, participation is felt as a fairly pleasant, good and true reality.

In Le Bouedec's study, factor dimensions were explicity oriented by different modalities of attitude scales because the latter contributed statistically to their formation. We may therefore conclude that the field's semantic elements are organized implicitly by their evaluative and, to a lesser extent, potency connotations. It should be noted, however, that the author treated separately the similarity relationship between words and the ratings of these words on different scales. Even if the two factor spaces are close to each other, it is not certain that the orientation of the factors determined by the similarities coincides with that communicated to the axes by the ratings of concepts. To solve this problem, it is necessary to use CFA and to project passive variables or modalities on to the space, i.e. modalities that do not take a role on computations for axis formation (see Part Three). By treating the ratings of concepts or the similarity relationship in this manner, it would be possible to verify the equivalence between the similarity relationship and the ratings on attitude scales.

Interpretation of Dimensions

Unlike the method used in the above illustration, the interpretation of dimensions in MDS does not result from the statistical orientation of the dimensional space. It requires finding directions from correlations between these dimensions and ratings of the elements located on these dimensions. In the present case, a stronger hypothesis is formulated in the relations between the proximities of the elements and their evaluative connotations.

Illustration: Intra-group Variability

To illustrate one way of giving a direction to the field dimensions obtained by MDS, we will take an example from subjects' perception of ingroup members. The procedure which we will describe is similar to that of Rosenberg and Sedlack (1972), discussed above.

We will briefly describe a study in which subjects (sixty-five apprentice craftsmen) were instructed to locate, by means of circles in a framework, nine ingroup members whom they had pre-identified by their initials. In addition to these nine individuals, the subjects were also asked to position themselves in the framework. The circles were to be entered according to the perceived proximity between individuals. Prior to this task, the subjects rated these individuals on the following five five-point scales: *intelligent, hard-working, typical of the ingroup, similar to the self* and *relations with the self.* The subjects rated themselves on the first three scales.

MDS was performed on the Euclidean distances between the different targets entered into the framework and identified by the numbers assigned to them by the subjects. A two-dimensional space provided a satisfactory fit to data (stress = 0.11). To interpret the dimensions thus obtained, we used a procedure similar to that employed by Rosenberg, Nelson and Vivekananthan (1968) and Rosenberg and Sedlack (1972).

The procedure was as follows (cf. Kruskal and Wish, 1976). We first aggregated the individual scores on the five scales for the nine individuals – ten for the first three scales – entered into the framework. We then performed a multiple regression analysis (MRA) for each of these variables by entering as independent variables the co-ordinates of each individual on the two dimensions. The multiple correlation coefficient showed us to what extent the dimensions, allowed us to account for the mean position of the targets on different scales, while the Beta coefficients enabled us to determine with which of the dimensions the scores on the scales were most correlated. We were thus able to give a meaning to the dimensions, or at least to one of them. It should be noted that the

Table 4.1   *Results of MRA of dimensions on five scales: multiple correlations and Beta coefficients*

Scale	Multiple R	Beta Dimension 1	Dimension 2
Intelligent	0.726 p<0.07	0.678	0.278
Hard-working	0.487 n.s		
Typical of ingroup	0.458 n.s.		
Similar to self	0.923 p<0.005	0.512	0.781
Relations with self	0.967 p<0.0005	0.445	0.871

Note: The Beta coefficients are very close to simple correlations because the two dimensions are virtually independent.

multiple correlations must be high in order to perform this operation. In our example, the results are shown in Table 4.1.

As shown in Table 4.1, the best correlation with the dimensional space was provided by the scales on which subjects rated others in comparison with themselves. These scales enabled mainly the second dimension to be interpreted by showing that the more the individuals were nega-

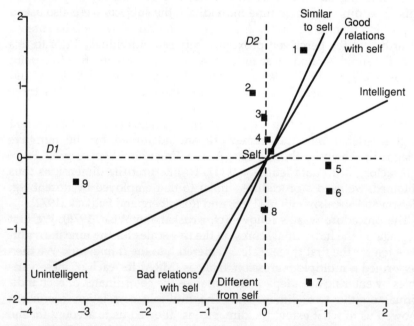

Figure 4.1   Graphic representation of dimension 1 and 2 of MDS on the representation of distances between nine ingroup members and self and projection of the straight lines of regression of evaluations of the members on three scales

Note: The ingroup members are numbered from 1 to 9.

tively positioned on this dimension, the smaller their similarity with the self and the worse their relations with the self. It should be noted that the scale *intelligent* – whose multiple correlation was too low for this scale alone to be used to interpret the dimensional space – tended to be correlated rather with the first dimension. As shown by the graphic representation below, the first dimension clearly opposed an individual – the last entered into the framework – to the others. On the other hand, the individuals spread out on the second dimension from the first named to the last. For building the graph by projecting the straight lines of regression, the reader is referred to Kruskal and Wish (1976, 35ff).

This method enables us to test the fact that subjects differentiate between ingroup members by referring to several dimensions simultaneously or to only one of them. The results presented here tend to show that the distribution of the ingroup members in a space is organized mainly by the relationship which subjects claim to have with each of them. They can be compared with certain works on the homogeneity of categories, particularly the approach of Marques, who showed that ingroup favouritism would be based on a more contrasting view of ingroup members than of outgroup members (Marques, Yzerbyt and Leyens, 1988). Such results also show the importance of the self in the perception of others as a sort of reference point. On this observation, we agree with Codol's works on the self as a reference target in a comparison with others (Codol, 1986).

Statistical Structure and Objectification

Statistical and Psychological Relations

Just as the study of SRs cannot be limited to objectification, field definition cannot be assimilated to a space of words defined by statistical relations. Geometrical and statistical links must not be confused with semantic and psychological links (Johnson and Wall, 1969; Funck, *et al.*, 1976). According to Funck *et al.* (p.128), the Euclidean representation, aesthetic and satisfactory though it is,

> lends no support to the hypothesis that the cognitive space is homologous to Euclidean metrics [. . .] One of the reasons for this belief is that the Euclidean model enables us to represent a 'cognitive map' easily and – if this map has any psychological reality – in a manner accessible to the human eye. One does not 'discover' that the cognitive structure is Euclidean, but one 'discovers' the nature of this structure through the filter of Euclidean metrics.

And the authors went on to assert that imposing this metrics may actually make it difficult to understand the psychosocial processes underlying individual judgements. By opening the conclusion of Part One with this warning, we do not mean to discourage researchers from using the above-described techniques (HCA, MDS and CFA). Quite the contrary. However, we must emphasize that the use of a statistical approach, however rigorous it may be, is effective only if it accompanies a consequent theoretical problem.

As far as objectification is concerned, it appears that defining the subject matter of a study is an essential first step. Without this preliminary work, building up survey material may well be like an empiricist operation from which scarcely any conclusion can be drawn. After recalling this basic point, we would like to stress the limits of an approach to SRs that considers only objectification. The first of these limits is due to the fact of asserting the existence of a central structure, a basic framework or a stable or even invariant fund of SRs. Admittedly, SRs are created in communication relationships that presuppose a language common to the subjects involved in these exchanges. One may therefore seek to define the components of this common basis and the way it is organized. One may even go further and seek to weight the importance of the components according to their frequency of occurrence, emotional meaning or other criteria. But this work would be incomplete if it did not reveal variations in these common bases. If one disregards the fact that, for one thing, objectification is only a framework shared by individuals and thus already modulated by individual differences and that, for another, these individuals position themselves in this framework according to their memberships in social groups, one is led to treat SRs only from a consensual angle. Parts Two and Three will deal with this aspect.

The second limit concerns field reification. Objectification is a dynamic process that cannot be apprehended statically. On the contrary: it must be made part of the evolutions that undergo symbolic exchanges. For example, it is important to ponder the question of actualizing learned discourses on everyday thinking and the return effects of this thinking on such discourses. To tackle this kind of question, one can use the analytic techniques (and the questionings to which they refer) discussed in Part One. We think it more judicious, however, to use other means of treating field variations, as we will see later.

Status of Field Dimensions

In fact, our above illustrations of organized central structures of SRs allow us to consider that, in a certain culture, individuals classify certain pieces of information according to common dimensions. In view of the warning given above, what status must be given to these dimensions? Must they be associated with the indirect methods or distortions mentioned by some authors when dealing with the cognitive functioning of individuals (cf. Nisbett and Ross, 1980)? We think it more correct to associate them with information-transforming processes of which these indirect methods are precisely the indicators – processes typical of common thinking. According to Moscovici (1986; Moscovici and Hewstone, 1984), when we look at individuals and objects,

> when we explain their characteristics, we 'forget' that they could be representations of another nature. We apply to them the categories of our social group and our acquired thought processes, and we combine them within this framework to make them just as we see them. And we cannot escape these categories or these thought processes characteristic of our representations any more than we can escape the laws of our anatomy and physiology. The result is that the contents and rules of this representative thinking end up forming around us an environment in which the physical and the social merge. (1984, 566)

The dimensions would constitute, in a way, major reference points shared by individuals of a social group because they apply the same rules for apprehending it. Personalization, representation and naturalization would be some of the arguments which we formulate in a stable and continuous way and which would lead us to build common semantic or logical classes.

PART II

Shared Knowledge and Individual Positions

What role do individual differences or heterogeneities play in the study of SRs?

Part One has shown how researchers infer the existence of SRs and compose them, in a way, from sets of individual responses. This involved forming coherent wholes from partial and varied contributions. Up to this point, however, the study of SRs emphasized consensus and thus missed some of their fundamental characteristics. SRs acquire their specificity only through their anchoring in the dynamics of symbolic relations between social actors, either interpersonal relations or relations between groups of individuals. The theory requires SRs to be studied at both the interpersonal and the collective levels. The techniques described in Part One treated SRs as if they were a system of structured contents shared by all individuals of a collective. The answers from an entire sample of individuals were mixed so that individual differences disappear in this procedure. However, dealing with the anchoring of SRs as a first step involves reintroducing the idea of inter-individual variation. In fact, as mentioned in the introduction to this book, the theory of SRs by no means rules out that individuals differ in their relationships with these representations. If one regards, as do certain researchers, representations as opinions, attitudes or stereotypes, one may conceive that individuals differ in the degree of their adherence to these different types of beliefs. If one considers, however, that representations are, above all, organizing principles that regulate symbolic relations, one can accept that this organization generates systematic inter-individual and inter-group differences and variations. Various multidimensional techniques enable these organizing principles to be studied. Part Two deals with inter-individual variation. In Part Three, we will further enrich the model by introducing group variations.

In fact, the use of multidimensional techniques is based on variations or heterogeneities. We will therefore discuss the way various multidimensional techniques treat, each in its specific way, inter-individual and/or inter-response differences.

In this Part we draw a distinction between two approaches of individual variations. The first approach is based on the correlation coefficient, and it is grounded in the application of factor analytic models. Factor analysis provides, among others, a measure of the specific *positioning* or locations of the individuals on dimensions of interrelated responses (i.e. factor scores). The second approach introduces an alternative measure of the sample variation in terms of the individuals' *uses* of each dimension (i.e. individual weights). In this latter case, the dimensions usually comprise a set of responses on one pole and another set of responses on the other pole. The weights correspond to the importance or saliency of such bipolar dimension for an individual. This approach is usually based on matrices of similarities or distances between responses, and it follows from the application of a technique named INDSCAL (individual differences model, a technique less commonly used by psychologists).

There are a number of other differences between factor analysis and INDSCAL. Some of them, as well as the most adequate applications of both techniques, are dealt with in the following chapters. However, despite critical differences, these approaches share an important property. As a matter of fact, the accurate usage of both techniques requires a homogeneous population of individuals. This implies that the variation in the sample should not be systematically accounted for by extraneous (and relevant) variables, for instance the sex of subjects or their experimental memberships. The object under study in this Part will therefore be the organization of inter-individual, and not intergroup, variations.

By analyzing specific kinds of individual variations, we move a step further in the quantitative study of social representations. Conceptions of social representations as consensual wholes will be challenged. The emphasis will be placed on the study of social representations as organizing principles of differences in individual positioning and individual weighting of dimensions. Paradoxically, analysis of social representations involves the investigation of areas of dissent on the importance of some issues, as well as on the stands that individuals take.

We will begin by describing three types of variation that may characterize individual responses to a given number of questions.

5

Three Basic Notions in the Multivariate Approach to Individual Differences:
Level, Dispersion and Correlation

Any distribution of responses on several variables can be statistically broken down into three elements: (1) level (mean of individual responses), (2) dispersion (degree of scattering of individual responses around the mean) and (3) correlation (link between individual responses for two variables, that is, the profile). These components represent as many viewpoints on data. Above all, it is the nature of the adopted viewpoint that characterizes a given technique (see Bacher, 1982, 300ff).

An illustration of these three characteristics of the distributions of responses is provided by Table 5.1. It shows four specific cases representing each of the distributions of three variables (called *V1*, *V2* and *V3*) measured on four individuals (ind.1 to ind.4).

In case 1, as in case 4, the means of three variables differ. However, the correlations between these variables are identical. In case 4, the dispersion varies from the single to the double according to the variables without affecting the correlations. Moreover, as indicated by case 3, the dispersions are not associated with the means, either. In case 2, however, there is no variation in level or dispersion, while the correlations differ widely. Variables *V1* and *V2* in case 2 comprise the same figures, if the successive order of individuals (values of 40 and 60) is not taken into account. By taking the successive order into account, which is done by the correlation as a measure of the inter-profile links, it appears that by progressing from individual 1 to individual 2, variable *V1* decreases (from 60 to 40), while variable *V2* increases (from 40 to 60). One thus notices that values, which are identical (or very similar) but arranged differently, affect only the correlations. These examples illustrate the independent nature of the three elements of the distributions. This characteristic enables us to predict that the correlation of –1 in case 2 would not be affected by any linear transformation of one of the two variables (e.g. addition of a constant to all the values of a variable; such a transformation would modify only the level of this variable). MDS will make

Table 5.1 *Four cases of different relations between levels, dispersions and correlations of three variables measured on four individuals.*

	Cases											
	1			2			3			4		
Ind.	V1	V2	V3	V1	V2	V3	V1	V2	V3	V1	V2	V3
1	20	40	60	60	40	60	40	35	30	60	35	10
2	40	60	80	40	60	60	60	65	70	80	65	50
3	20	40	60	40	60	40	40	35	30	60	35	10
4	40	60	80	60	40	40	60	65	70	80	65	50
Mean	30	50	70	50	50	50	50	50	50	70	50	30
SD	10	10	10	10	10	10	10	15	20	10	15	20

	Correlations											
	V1	V2	V3	V1	V2	V3	V1	V2	V3	V1	V2	V3
V1	1			1			1			1		
V2	1	1		-1	1		1	1		1	1	
V3	1	1	1	0	0	1	1	1	1	1	1	1

Note: Mean = Mean (level)
SD= Standard deviation (dispersion)
(Adapted from Carroll and Field, 1974)

full use of this characteristic of the distributions.

Level, dispersion and profile or correlation may, however, establish links of dependence for primarily empirical reasons. Such is the case, for example, when a 'ceiling effect' marks individual responses to items of scales. In this case, the levels of two variables rise, while their dispersions diminish (respondents have a limited range of possible responses available at the extremities of the scales) and the link between their profiles becomes closer. Other examples going beyond the strict limits of the scales are halo and social-desirability effects. These phenomena usually come under the heading of indirect questioning methods and can usually be only partly circumvented by means of statistical analysis such as analysis of covariance (for systematic treatment of these indirect methods, see Poulton, 1989).

Various multidimensional approaches may be classified according to the element (or elements) of the distributions which they enable us to examine: individual profiles of responses, variations and distances between responses of different persons, mean degree of agreement with suggested responses.

6
Factor Analysis:
Individual Positions in the Representational Field

Thus, factor analysis, (or multiple regression analysis, to be described later) is generally used to summarize the variations in a representational field for a given population. This technique closely examines the links between profiles of individual responses in this population but not the level and dispersion of these responses. To make up for it, other techniques such as MDS or HCA (see Part One) aim to account for relations between responses through mean distances between stimuli. Generally, these stimuli have been rated by a relatively homogeneous population of subjects (questions arising from the heterogeneity of the study population will be treated in Part Three). Finally, INDSCAL (individual differences multidimensional scaling), a special technique halfway between the two above-mentioned approaches, will be explained later in Part Two. In summary, the main difference between these techniques lies in the type of information analyzed. It is therefore very important for the user to know the rules of application and interpretation of the analytic method chosen. We will begin by considering factor analysis.

Factor Analysis: Covariations and Heterogeneity of Responses

By factor analysis, one means a large family of techniques whose common denominator is to investigate covariations between response profiles. Beyond this summary definition, factor-analytic methods differ widely in their characteristics. The differences lie in the consideration of total variance (principal-component analysis) or of single variance common to all variables (factor analysis), the analyzed units (responses in general, but also individuals in some cases), the type of correlation coefficient used (the most popular being Pearson correlation) and the conception of the factor structure (factor rotations towards a simple

structure of orthogonal or oblique type). We will briefly discuss the
main concepts of factor analysis (for a non-technical discussion of the
characteristics of this technique, see, for instance, Rummel, 1974;
Comrey, 1978). Proposed examples will then illustrate some applications
of this technique in the study of SRs.

Various Models of Factor Analysis

We will first make a basic distinction between two widely used specific
factor-analytic techniques: (1) principal-component factor analysis which
can be compared to CFA, and (2) common-variance factor analysis.

Principal-component analysis (PCA) reproduces the total variation of a
large number of variables (ten to forty in most cases) in a smaller number of dimensions (two to six in general). The sample population of individuals must be at least as large as the number of variables, but prefer-
ably four to five times larger, if possible. PCA *reduces* initial data and
inevitably causes some loss of information compared with individual
responses. In compensation, it provides a well structured and readily
accessible view of the way variables covary, oppose each other or are
independent of each other. The algorithm proceeds by extracting dimensions (these dimensions are also called factors; this term should, however, be reserved for products of common-variance factor analysis). The
loading of each variable on each dimension, which is defined as a correlation between the variable and this dimension, indicates the contribution of the variable to the dimension in question. The loadings are all the
higher as the corresponding variables help give a meaning to the dimension. The square of a loading provides the percentage of common variance in the corresponding variable which is explained by the dimension
(thus, a loading of 0.80 indicates that 64 per cent of the variation in the
variable is explained by the dimension). To interpret dimensions, one
generally considers only the loadings of +/–0.30 (which corresponds to
about 10 per cent of variance explained). The sign of loading is an
important element for the examination of bivariate correlations. Two
variables with loadings of the same sign (positive or negative) on a
dimension covary on this dimension. If the loadings have opposite
signs, they contribute in an opposite manner to the meaning of the
dimension. There are usually three types of dimensions (or factors, as
this applies just as well to common-variance factor analysis). The first
dimension describes the main direction of the network of correlations.
This dimension is usually an overall factor on which all variables have
positive and relatively high loadings. It thus describes a source of variation going through the whole study population: the dimension is present in all individuals, but to varying degrees, which is an important fact

to remember. Let us imagine, for example, that individuals have to describe themselves with a series of traits on intensity scales. Usually, the first dimension extracted is an overall dimension. This dimension can be interpreted as an indication of individuals' propensity to describe themselves positively by giving a 'good' image of themselves. Self-enhancement thus increases positive correlations between different traits enhanced in the same direction. Positive self-description by subjects on the scales is responsible for this increase in the correlations between scales. One may therefore conclude that this propensity for positive self-description is a characteristic of the study population. However, this conclusion does not imply that all individuals enhance themselves to the same extent. The heterogeneity of the mean levels of self-enhancement is, on the contrary, a condition for the appearance of this overall dimension. The successive dimensions will be either group dimensions or specific. The group dimensions are composed of two or more variables that covary on a dimension. When positive and negative signs are present on the same dimension, one talks of bipolar (as opposed to unipolar) group factors. This is often the case, for instance, when self-descriptions concern maleness or femaleness scales. These two types of scales will stand out on a bipolar dimension: the more the individuals assume male traits, the more they reject (or the less they accept) female traits, and vice versa. In the end, specific factors are those that comprise only high loadings for a variable at one and the same time. Usually, the user discontinues the analysis before such dimensions appear.

Common-variance factor analysis is a classic factor-analytic model. This technique describes the common variation in a set of variables. Factors may be considered to be sources of variation (or causes) underlying all variables. In theoretical terms, therefore, the basic difference from the previous models is that the variation extracted by this analysis concerns only what is common to all the analyzed variables. In practical terms, it follows that hypotheses or expectations should be systematically formulated concerning the factors thus obtained and the characteristics of these factors (their predictive field in particular). The extreme case of this approach is represented by confirmatory factor analysis (often performed through the LISREL program). This type of analysis, however, has yet to be successfully used in the SR field. The aim of PCA is, by contrast, purely descriptive (see in this connection Thurstone (1955) on the debates at the French Scientific Research Center).

Factor Scores

Often, researchers are interested in the position of individual respondents on each of the extracted factors. *Factor scores* provide these positions. Each extracted factor yields a variable of factor scores. Each individual will thus have a value on each of these variables. This value will indicate, for the factor in question, the extent to which each respondent participates in the meaning provided by the dimension. Factor scores are new variables that can be used, after performing factor analysis, to examine the responses of individuals in connection with other characteristics of these individuals (one can, for instance, test if individuals with high scores on a 'maleness–femaleness' dimension differ from those with low scores concerning their self-esteem).

Factor analysis also involves 'decision making' by the user. Decisions must be made at different stages of the analysis. The most common decision-making problems concern the number of factors or dimensions to be chosen and the different factor-rotating techniques to be used.

Concerning the number of dimensions, various criteria are available, with the final criterion being chosen empirically. Some specialists think that the interpretability of dimensions themselves is a valid criterion that determines when to stop extracting further dimensions (see Schiffman, Reynolds and Young, 1981). The extracted factors appear in the order corresponding to the amount of variation explained, from the most potent to the least potent. The eigenvalue indicates the amount of variance extracted and corresponds to the sum of loadings on a factor after their squaring. Since the variables are automatically standardized by calculating correlations, the variance of each analyzed variable is worth '1'. Thus, an eigenvalue of five in an analysis comprising twenty variables means that the dimension corresponding to this eigenvalue represents 25 per cent of total variation. One usually considers that factor analysis should account for at least 40 per cent of variance. One way to solve the problem of the number of factors is therefore to select all the factors corresponding to an eigenvalue at least equal to 1 (i.e. summing up the variation of at least a single variable).

Interpreting the factors requires both methodological and practical knowledge (as will be shown, using examples). To facilitate this interpretation, many procedures for 'rotating the factors toward a simple structure' have been devised. The rotation is designed to simplify the structure of loadings on different extracted dimensions. The most popular rotation technique, called 'varimax' (variance maximum), produces the following effects on extracted dimensions: each variable will have near-zero correlations on all factors except one. Each factor will comprise only a limited number of variables with high correlations. This technique respects inter-dimensional orthogonality (statistical independence). Other techniques, called 'oblique rotation', will produce inter-correlated factors. Interpreting them becomes more difficult, however. These techniques are therefore used less often.

We will now give two examples of the use of factor analysis. We will particularly illustrate the validity of distinguishing between analyses of mean levels of responses and analyses of correlations between response profiles. For the second example, we will discuss regression analysis that will allow us to conclude that a given organizing principle is more deeply involved than others in the modulation of individual differences in relation to a SR.

Finally, we will show that factor analysis can also be used when the questioning method severely limits the variation in responses from one and the same subject. This is the case, for instance, when a subject has to arrange his/her preferences for a series of objects. Inevitably, expressing a first choice limits the options for the remaining objects as well as for the second choice and so on. One talks then of ipsative measurements.

Illustration: Representations of Psychologists' Work

This example is based on a series of studies of representations of psychologists' work conducted in Italy and Switzerland (Palmonari, 1981; Doise *et al.*, 1982; De Paolis, Lorenzi-Cioldi and Pombeni, 1983; Palmonari and Zani, 1989). It enables us to deal easily with the complex structure of homogeneities and differences in the use of factor analysis.

Initially, four types of representations were obtained by analyzing the thematic and typologic content of a series of interviews. We will describe these types of representations only briefly here, because a more detailed description is found in the questionnaire we compiled with the help of our Italian colleagues.

Type A explicitly subordinates the legitimacy of psychologists' activity to their political commitment. Solely a political action that would transform today's society can enable psychologists, who regard themselves as social workers like others, to engage in an activity that does not alienate people or mask the true problems of our society.

Type B attaches great importance to the integration of psychologists' work into an inter-disciplinary undertaking. The representatives of this type also advocate social change. To make this change, however, analyses and joint actions of different social-science specialists are required. The specific contribution of psychologists is essential to such joint undertakings.

Type C, unlike the above two types, stresses the independent nature of the work of psychologists who have theoretical and technical tools for solving individual and inter-individual problems. The individual and inter-individual relationships are specific areas of psychologists' work.

Type D bases psychologists' activity on their personal qualities essential for having successful relationships with their clients or patients. Advocates of this view of psychological practice often claim to be inspired by various psychotherapeutic approaches. The individual's well-being is the ultimate goal of psychologists' work.

These four types of representations might be named more concisely: political militant, inter-disciplinarian, technician and clinician. Obviously, however, these names alone cannot identify the different types.

These four types do not seem to appear with equal frequency in the different social milieux studied in Italy. Type A is said to have been especially present when sector psychology was introduced recently. Type D is particularly widespread among those who practise a liberal profession and some academics. When public institutions age, types B and C are said to appear more frequently.

This typology seems by no means strange to those who are familiar with the discussions that have been going on among psychologists since the late 1960s in various European countries. But one also needs a handier tool for verifying the relevance of the typology described in other countries, or even in Italy itself. A questionnaire was thus compiled. For each of the fourteen aspects (or headings) of psychologists' professional activity extracted by content analysis, four propositions (items) were formulated to match the four types of representations described above. Generally, statements extracted from conversations directly inspired the formulation of questionnaire items. The four items of each heading were presented randomly in the questionnaire. Care was taken to ensure that items concerning one and the same heading did not follow each other too closely and that the questionnaire did not begin with propositions considered 'extreme'. The definitive compilation of the questionnaire was then finalized by mutual agreement between Italian and Swiss researchers in both French and Italian versions.

Table 6.1 shows, by way of example, eight items that correspond to types A, B, C and D for two different headings (the reader may refer to the above-mentioned publications for the unabridged version of the questionnaire). For each item, subjects were asked to indicate the degree of their agreement or disagreement on a four- or five-point scale depending on studies (scales ranging from −2 for disagreement to +2 for agreement). We will consider below the use of four-point scales (1 to 4; Table 6.1 shows, in parentheses, the mean observed in the sample population of Swiss students).

A summary of a study conducted with Swiss students (Doise *et al.*, 1982) will serve to illustrate the main results of these investigations. The results of the Italian study (De Paolis, Lorenzi-Cioldi and Pombeni, 1983) were identical with those of the Swiss study on the essential points.

An analysis of the items in terms of means shows that most subjects accepted most of type B and C items, but that they generally rejected type A items. By contrast, type D items were partly accepted and partly

Table 6.1   *Questionnaire items corresponding to two of 14 headings*

Heading: aim of psychology

Type A:	Psychology is often used to divert attention from the true social problems facing individuals (1.99).
Type B:	Psychology enables us to know more about social reality in which individuals live (3.04).
Type C:	Psychology enables us to get to know the individual and his/her relationship with others better (3.43).
Type D:	Psychology may help individuals know themselves better (3.35).

Heading: definition of intervention

Type A:	Psychologists as such cannot change social reality (3.18).
Type B:	Psychologists' specific skills combined with those of other social-science specialists are needed to work out any program of social change (3.15).
Type C:	Psychologists' activity should aim primarily at changing the individual and his/her relationship with others (2.51).
Type D:	Psychologists' activity should aim primarily at ensuring the individual's well-being (3.43).

Note: 4-point scale: 1 = disagreement
                    4 = agreement

On the right of each item is the mean score of the responses of eighty Swiss subjects.

rejected (see Table 6.2).

As shown in Table 6.2, the items of 'intermediate' types received the highest level of acceptance, while the items of extreme types, especially type A, were massively rejected. One may therefore conclude that types B and C are the opposite of types A and D as regards their acceptance 'levels'. In various studies, factor analysis of fifty-six items consistently revealed two unipolar factors exhibiting the positive covariation of types A and B (factor 1) and types C, D and B (factor 2). Table 6.3 summarizes the loadings of the analysis of the Swiss students.

We are thus faced with the apparent inconsistency of the results obtained by two statistical approaches: analysis of means (levels) of agreement on the one hand, and analysis of correlations (profiles) on the other seem to lead to different interpretations.

Let us first take the results of factor analysis. The factor scores indicate the position of each respondent on the factors. Does this mean that all individuals with positive and high scores on the first factor, for example, accepted type A and B items? An examination of Table 6.2 suggests a

Table 6.2 *Number of massively accepted or rejected types A, B, C and D items*

	Items	
	Rejected	Accepted
Type		
A	7	1
B	1	8
C	2	8
D	6	4

(Doise et al., 1982, 198)

negative response in so far as type A items were massively rejected, while type B items were mostly accepted. These individuals may have generally rejected fewer type A items and accepted more type B items than did other individuals.

To understand better the reasoning underlying the interpretation of the results on the representation of psychologists' work, let us imagine the following example that shows the responses of six individuals to four items: two items – A1 and A2 – of type A, an item – B1 – of type B and an item – C1 – of type C. Table 6.4 lists the four items. The items are numbered according to their use in the example that will follow. This table shows the mean degree of agreement observed in the sample population of Swiss students.

Table 6.5 shows, by way of example, the responses of six fictitious individuals to these items. The responses are none the less compatible with the results obtained from the real population.

One finds that items A1 and A2 are consensually rejected (respective means: 1.33 and 1.67), while items B1 and C1 are consensually accepted (respective means: 3.50 and 3.67). The means (levels) of the first two items therefore differ widely from the other two. The correlations between the responses to the items are given in Table 6.6.

As one can see, A1 and A2, which have similar means, are positively

Table 6.3 *Number of items of each type (A, B, C and D) with significant positive or negative loadings on the first two factors*

	Factor			
	1		2	
	Negative	Positive	Negative	Positive
Type				
A	1	9	1	0
B	2	7	0	7
C	2	3	0	8
D	1	3	0	8

(Doise et al., 1982, 201)

Table 6.4 *Mean responses to three types of items*

Heading: relations with other disciplines

Type A	(A1 in our example): Any psychological research and intervention should be based on political analyses (1.53).
Type B	(B1 in our example): Any psychological research and intervention should take into account the acquired knowledge of other social sciences (3.56).

Heading: relations between public and private sectors

Type A	(A2 in our example): Psychologists' work should always be performed at a public institution (1.99).

Heading: definitions of psychological intervention

Type C	(C1 in our example): Psychologists should endeavour to broaden their knowledge and improve various techniques to help the individual and facilitate inter-individual relationships (3.30).

Note: 4-point scale: 1 = disagreement
4 = agreement

correlated. But B1 and C1, which also have similar means, are negatively correlated. One also notes, however, that A1 (or A2) and B1, which have very different means, are correlated positively and substantially (0.71). Thanks to the small number of individuals involved, a simple look at their responses enables us to understand this phenomenon: when agreement with item B1 increases (e.g. from 3 to 4 by progressing from the first to the second individual), disagreement with item A1 (or A2) decreases. The positive sign of correlation, while the two items elicit opposite responses, derives from a simple statistical characteristic of the

Table 6.5 *Responses of six fictitious individuals to four items of different types*

	Items			
	A1	A2	B1	C1
Individual				
1	1	1	3	4
2	2	2	4	3
3	1	2	3	4
4	1	2	4	3
5	2	2	4	4
6	1	1	3	4

Note: 4-point scale: 1 = disagreement
4 = agreement

Table 6.6   *Correlations between three types of items*

	A1	A2	B1	C1
A1	1.00			
A2	0.50	1.00		
B1	0.71	0.71	1.00	
C1	−0.25	−0.50	−0.71	1.00

correlations. As mentioned above, means (or frequencies) on the one hand and correlations on the other measure aspects of the distributions that are distinct from and independent of each other, i.e. their level (intensity) and profile (covariation) respectively.

Let us now factor-analyze the responses to the four items and calculate the factor scores of the six fictitious individuals. Of course, using factor analysis makes little sense for such a limited number of variables, but the argument can be extended to cover actual cases. Table 6.7 shows the results.

We find that type A items covary on the factor with type B items. This factor is interpreted correctly as the concomitant variation in items A1, A2 and B1. This covariation is, however, independent of the levels of item acceptance or rejection. This result reflects the response structuring obtained on the first factor of the factor analysis of research on psychologists. In this research, too, the positive covariation in the responses to type A and B items is due to the fact that both types referred, to varying degrees, to psychologists' political action. Since type A items are too extreme, however, subjects have rejected them all. By contrast, type B items, moderate, have been accepted. It is therefore very important to note that factor analysis alone can reveal the force and size of a 'social-versus-personal' dimension in the representations of psychologists' work. This is not possible by simply studying acceptance levels.

Table 6.7   *Factor matrix (loadings of variables on factor 1) and factor scores of six individuals on this factor*

Variable	Factor 1
A1	0.75
A2	0.83
B1	0.96
C1	−0.75
Individual	**Factor Score**
1	−1.07
2	1.23
3	−0.48
4	0.70
5	0.70
6	−1.07

Let us further examine the results of our fictitious example. Item C1 appears on the opposite pole of the factor and thus separates from type A and B items. Let us recall, however, that in terms of analysis of means, this item is similar to B1. This apparent inconsistency of the results can be interpreted, similarly to the preceding case, by examining raw data. We thus see a negative covariation appear between the responses given to items C1 and B1.

The factor scores of our fictitious example are organized along this unipolar factor with individuals 2, 4 and 5 having positive scores and individuals 1, 3 and 6 having negative scores. Individuals 4 and 5, who have identical factor scores, have none the less different responses. In fact, the individuals placed at the positive pole of the dimension opposing types A and B to type C are simply those who adhere to type B most firmly and reject type A least categorically. At this stage, we rediscover the reasoning based on the intensity of responses. But the described response behaviour makes sense only with respect to a correct interpretation of the factor dimension. This dimension respects, in this case, the heterogeneity of individual responses, while all variables of the A and B type covary positively.

In conclusion, the factor analysis of the representations of psychologists' work has shown that the political field, although massively rejected, is a powerful response-structuring factor. Factor dimensions indicate that, when subjects moderately reject the extreme positions conveyed by type A items, significant configurations appear associating other items (type B in particular) which also take into account aspects that are not immediately political.

The example of psychologists' work illustrates how factor analysis apprehends organizing principles at work in SRs. In specific cases, it is the most massively rejected items that, far from being irrelevant, best organize the field of representations of psychologists' work.

Factor Analysis and Multiple Regression Analysis: Modulation of the Role of Organizing Principles

Illustration: Causes of Delinquency

Another example of the importance of the interplay of variations for apprehending the organization of inter-individual differences was provided by a study by Doise and Papastamou (1987). This example will show that it is especially the positions diverging from those of most group members in a major area (belief in a biological explanation for criminality) that enable us to predict, in specific cases, the recourse to other types of reductionistic explanations.

This research involved ninety-five first-year psychology students. Its aim was to study the students' beliefs about the causes of delinquency and the way of 'handling' delinquents and to examine the role of these beliefs in their reactions to specific cases.

To apprehend general beliefs about the causes of delinquency, we used a questionnaire that had already proved useful for studying these beliefs in another student population. To this questionnaire, we added a set of items for general opinions on the way our society handles delinquents: imprisonment and psychiatric care. A second questionnaire focused on the way the same students reacted to more specific cases of minor delinquency and more specifically on the degree of acceptance of different but highly 'reductionistic' explanations. These explanations attributed each time a single cause to account for individual behaviour that may be thought to fit into a fabric of multiple determinisms. The items of both questionnaires represented positions that are common in criminality literature, and they were prepared on the basis of discussions with jurists and psychologists.

The two questionnaires therefore differed from each other in that the first dealt with delinquency in general, while the second asked subjects to explain the criminal behaviour of a specific individual. The nature of this behaviour varied, in the sense that some offences were political protest acts, while others were offences against private property. Each subject had to explain four cases: two protest acts and two offences against private property. Each time, a student, a young man, an adult or a civil servant was described as a protagonist.

The first questionnaire asked subjects to answer (on a seven-point scale ranging from 1 = fully agree to 7 = fully disagree) two sets of questions: a first set of twelve questions concerning the cause of delinquency and a second set of twelve questions concerning the handling of delinquents (see Tables 6.8 and 6.9 for the content of these questions).

The second questionnaire ran to four pages. On each page was a brief description of a case. Example: 'A trainee civil servant was caught by the police in the act of covering the walls of a public building with anti-militaristic slogans'. After reading this presentation, subjects had to say why the author of the act in question behaved the way he did. To do so, they were asked to take a stand (on a seven-point scale) on fifteen different reductionistic explanations. Example: 'The author of this act behaved the way he did because he was psychologically unbalanced' or 'because he was dependent on his ideological options'. In fact, certain explanations proposed a psychological determinism, while others suggested a social determinism or even a hereditary or biological determinism (see Table 6.10 for the content of the questions).

Factor Analysis and Organizing Principles

Let us first examine the results obtained about the causes of delinquency.

Table 6.8 shows the means of responses as well as the results of factor analysis of the causes of 'delinquency in general'. Let us first note the most clear-cut agreements and the most categorical rejections. Three items obtained a high degree of agreement (means below 3). Criminal acts can be seen as acts of revolt (item 3), and their causes are to be sought in the personal history of delinquents (item 4) or in frustrations resulting from unsatisfactory interpersonal relationships (item 7). The most categorically rejected items (means above 5) attributed the causes of delinquency to organic characteristics of delinquents (item 1), the laws of heredity (item 8) and congenital mental abnormalities (item 10). Three factors were chosen by factor analysis (see Table 6.8). The first factor related to a social and economic explanation (social exploitation and inequality, socioeconomic system and recidivist-producing prison), the second to a biological explanation (the three most categorically rejected items summarized above) and the third to psychological explanations (frustrating interpersonal relationships and adolescent crisis).

Let us now consider the handling of delinquents. The items that obtained the highest degree of agreement (means below 3) asserted that

Table 6.8 *Causes of delinquency: mean responses and factor analysis results*

		Means	Factors 1	Factors 2	Factors 3	Communality
	Summary of items					
1.	Organic causes	5.77	−0.26	0.48	0.05	0.30
2.	Social origin	4.71	0.23	0.17	−0.14	0.10
3.	Acts of revolt	2.59	0.24	−0.18	0.21	0.14
4.	Personal history	2.39	−0.02	0.03	0.26	0.05
5.	Social exploitation	3.95	0.41	−0.04	−0.31	0.27
6.	Social inequality	3.08	0.66	−0.04	−0.14	0.46
7.	Interpersonal frustration	2.55	0.06	−0.11	0.49	0.26
8.	Laws of heredity	6.47	0.04	0.57	0.10	0.33
9.	Adolescent crisis	3.60	−0.01	0.02	0.77	0.58
10.	Congenital abnormalities	6.32	0.06	0.74	−0.18	0.59
11.	Socioeconomic system	3.16	0.59	−0.04	0.09	0.36
12.	Recidivists	3.18	0.43	0.00	0.16	0.20
Eigenvalues:			2.06	1.87	1.57	
% explained total variance			17.20	15.60	13.10	

Note: Scale used: 1 = Agreement
 7 = Disagreement

Table 6.9   *Handling of delinquents: mean responses and factor analysis results*

		Means		Loadings		
				Factors		Communality
			1	2	3	
	Summary of items					
1.	Therapy prevents delinquency	3.53	0.74	0.10	–0.02	0.56
2.	Imprisonment is effective	6.67	0.05	0.62	–0.05	0.39
3.	Therapy makes for irresponsibility	4.71	–0.32	0.17	–0.01	0.14
4.	Prison helps social rehabilitation	6.60	0.02	0.66	–0.05	0.44
5.	Therapy provides self-protection	4.14	0.44	0.08	–0.16	0.23
6.	Prison helps develop social awareness	5.20	0.03	0.64	–0.14	0.43
7.	Therapy and social integration	3.05	0.86	0.00	0.07	0.74
8.	Prison and social marginalization	2.43	0.11	–0.21	0.80	0.70
9.	Psychiatry relieves society	3.48	–0.21	–0.08	0.40	0.21
10.	Psychiatry better than examining magistrates	2.36	0.31	–0.05	0.36	0.23
11.	Psychiatrist's appraisal necessary	2.66	0.35	0.08	–0.10	0.14
12.	Psychiatry and marginalization	3.12	–0.13	0.01	0.38	0.16
Eigenvalues:			2.46	2.14	1.44	
% explained variance:			20.50	17.90	12.10	

Note: Scale used: 1 = Agreement
                    7 = Disagreement

prisons marginalize their inmates socially (item 8), that psychiatrists obtain more information than do examining magistrates (item 10) and that a psychiatrist's appraisal is necessary when the motives for a crime elude common sense (item 11). The most categorically rejected items (means above 5) described the prison as the only effective response to delinquents (item 2), as a means of their education and effective social rehabilitation (item 4) and as a way of making them realize the illegal nature of their acts (item 6).

Factor analysis again enabled three factors to be selected. The first factor was loaded with items asserting the efficacy of therapeutic handling in fighting delinquency (item 1), protecting delinquents from themselves

Table 6.10 *Explanation for specific cases: mean responses according to the nature of offences*

	Protest acts	Offences against property
Summary of items		
1. Psychological unbalance	6.36	5.42 **
2. Ideological options	3.13	6.05 **
3. Unhappy childhood	6.11	5.23 **
4. Disadvantaged social background	5.98	4.85 **
5. Desire to impress others	4.81	5.57 **
6. Desire to protest	1.80	5.21 **
7. Biological deficiencies	6.61	6.39 *
8. Precarious employment situation	5.94	5.33 **
9. Authoritarian parents	5.56	5.47
10. Extremist convictions	3.36	5.90 **
11. Mental instability	6.18	5.10 **
12. Attraction of the forbidden	5.19	4.79 *
13. Relationship problems	5.70	4.67 **
14. No social integration	4.91	4.63
15. Influence of bad examples	6.29	5.72 **

Note: Scale used: 1 = Agreement
  7 = Disagreement
t-Test: significance threshold of differences: * $p < 0.01$
  ** $p < 0.001$

(item 5) and integrating them socially (item 7). The second factor was loaded with the most categorically rejected items, all of which concerned the prison's role. The third factor was associated with an item denouncing the perverse role of both the prison (item 8) and psychiatry (item 9).

Several analyses were performed on the explanations given for specific cases. They all showed that the status of the actor (young man or student versus adult or civil servant) had little impact compared with more important elements such as the nature of offences: protest acts or offences against private property. This is why Table 6.10 groups the results obtained for these two types of offences by indicating each time the significance threshold between these means.

The items flatly rejected (means above 6) for explaining protest acts and less categorically rejected for explaining offences against private property were psychological unbalance (item 1), unhappy childhood (item 3), biological deficiencies (item 7), mental instability (item 11) and influence of bad examples (item 15). For four other items, the rejection was slightly less categorical but remained more categorical for explaining protest acts than for explaining offences against private property. These items were social origin (item 4), precarious employment situation (item 8), attraction of what is forbidden (item 12) and relationship problems (item 13).

Only four causes were more categorically rejected when explaining offences against private property than when explaining protest acts: ideological options (item 2), desire to impress others (item 5) or to commit a protest act (item 6) and extremist convictions (item 10). Three of these items (items 2, 6 and 10) were very close in their contents to protest acts. Our study population rejected reductionistic explanations for protest acts more categorically than those for offences against private property. Only two items failed to reveal any significant difference between these two types of acts: parental authoritarianism (item 9) and absence of social integration (item 14).

To conclude, let us add that most first-year psychology students rejected the reductionistic explanations, especially for protest acts. However, which of their general beliefs affected the degree of their rejection or acceptance of the reductionistic explanations for specific acts?

Use of Factor Scores in Multiple Regression Analysis

Factor analysis has taught us that easily recognizable organizing principles bearing upon environmentalist, hereditarian or psychologizing positions are at work in the structuring of general beliefs about the causes of delinquency. Other principles organize opinions on the handling of delinquents: therapy or the prison's role. But do all these general beliefs play the same role in the search for explanations when confronted with specific acts? To answer this question, we will simply report here the particularly clear-cut results of multiple regression analysis (MRA) ('step-by-step' method).

MRA (see Pedhazur, 1982, for an excellent introduction to this method) is a technique of explaining the variation in a dependent variable by means of several other independent variables. This explanation is based on analysis of correlations between these variables. One thus searches for the specific (or sole) contributions of each of the independent variables to the dependent variable. Using the 'step-by-step' method, the process of including independent variables is discontinued when the variables to be included no longer substantially help explain the variance in the dependent variable. MRA results are presented in the form of 'Beta' coefficients and are interpreted as the sole contributions of the variables to the variation of the dependent variable.

Let us revert to our example. MRA employed to explain specific cases of deviance involves as dependent variables the responses to the fifteen items for each of the four specific cases, which gives us sixty different analyses. The independent variables are the factor scores of each subject on the six factors (three for the causes of delinquency and three for the handling of delinquents) of the questionnaire on general opinions. The results show the vast superiority of the predictive value for the scores on the second causal factor – the one which is highly loaded with three 'hereditarian' items. In fact, thirty-five times the scores on this 'biological' factor are significantly related ($p<0.05$) to explanations for specific cases. No other factor obtains significant predictive links for more than four different items. Table 6.11 shows for which specific cases and for which items the scores on the 'biological' factor had a significant predictive value. Let us point out that all the links were positive: higher scores on the 'biological' factor predicted higher scores for all kinds of reductionistic explanations whose content often has no apparent connection with a hereditarian explanation.

One may wonder if these results were not due to a third variable that would be a sort of tendency to reject any statement in an extreme manner. Two indications oppose this interpretation: factor 2 of the analysis of the general questionnaire on the handling of delinquents was also highly loaded with items that were flatly rejected. These scores had only a low predictive value because they were significant only in three cases

Table 6.11   *Results of MRA of the explanation for specific cases: significance of the predictive value of the factor scores of the 'biological cause'*

	Protest acts		Offences against property	
	Students	Civil servants	Young men	Adult
Summary of items				
1. Psychological unbalance	0.01	0.01	0.001	n.s.
2. Ideological options	n.s.	n.s.	0.01	0.01
3. Unhappy childhood	n.s.	0.01	0.01	0.05
4. Disadvantaged background	n.s.	0.01	0.05	n.s.
5. Desire to impress others	0.01	0.001	n.s.	n.s.
6. Desire to protest	n.s.	n.s.	0.05	n.s.
7. Biological deficiencies	0.01	0.001	0.001	0.01
8. Precarious employment	n.s.	0.01	0.05	n.s.
9. Authoritarian parents	n.s.	0.05	0.05	0.05
10. Extremist convictions	n.s.	0.05	0.05	n.s.
11. Mental instability	0.001	0.001	0.001	n.s.
12. Attraction of the forbidden	0.01	0.01	n.s.	n.s.
13. Relationship problems	0.01	n.s.	0.01	n.s.
14. No social integration	n.s.	0.001	0.05	n.s.
15. Influence of bad examples	0.001	0.01	n.s.	n.s.

(items for offences against private property: once for a young man and twice for an adult). Moreover, the results did not change basically when two supplementary independent variables were entered: the scores of extreme responses to the questions about the causes of delinquency and the handling of delinquents. These scores of extreme responses had a predictive value in nine cases, but removed a predictive value from the scores of the 'biological' factor only in two out of thirty-five cases.

Let us summarize the contributions of this research. It enabled us first to find in first-year psychology students an easily interpretable organization of general beliefs about criminality. While the organizing principles of these beliefs were very clear, however, they were not all equally important for explaining differences of interpretation of specific cases of delinquency. 'Reductionistic' explanations for protest acts or offences against private property were rejected fairly categorically to the extent to which subjects rejected 'hereditarian' or 'biologizing' explanations for criminality in general. Other more 'environmentalist' or 'psychologizing' causal conceptions or general views about the handling of delinquents predicted the degree of acceptance of different explanations for specific cases much less. It was as if the relative acceptance of general 'hereditarian' or 'biologizing' explanations predisposed subjects to accept all sorts of other explanations for specific cases more easily.

As far as delinquency was concerned, most of our subjects had clear-cut opinions: they rejected simplistic and reductionistic explanations. As for general conceptions, they rejected, above all, deterministic explanations of a biological nature. However, some of our subjects, for reasons which our research failed to clarify, did not fully share this rejection, and they also rejected a whole set of explanations for specific cases less categorically. This would be a sort of disanchoring – the giving up of certain positions common to the members of a group entailing the abandonment of other positions. Our results showed that this did not mean abandonment or relaxation in any area. For instance, distancing oneself from the prevailing ideas about the prison's harmful role did not result in this generalized disanchoring. To explain these differential effects, it was necessary to resort to mechanisms similar to those described by Le Poultier (1986): it is individual-centred conceptions, notably explanations referring to the individual's hereditary or biological constitution, that account for the disanchoring process. Moreover, factors providing high loadings to items of a general nature on which opinions are divided (socioeconomic and relational factors) play a far less important part in the prediction of concrete explanations. These factors relate to more fluctuating opinions in the population: distancing oneself relatively from these opinions does not necessarily affect explanations for specific cases.

Factor Analysis of Repeated or Ipsative Measurements: Intra-individual Variations

It was Cattell who made a distinction between normative and ipsative measurements (1944). Normativity denotes the independence of two measurements made on the same individuals. The normative measurements comprise separate scales for each question. The respondent population is therefore distributed around the mean of responses to each scale. Thus, the responses of an individual to two questions about his/her opinion are metrically independent of each other, since the individual can establish any links between scores on these two questions. Let us make it clear, however, that this metric independence by no means implies the psychological independence of observations. Ipsativity, on the contrary, denotes the dependence of measurements. Two questions are ipsative when answering one of the questions depends on answering the other question. This is the case, for instance, when subjects are asked to order two SR items according to the degree of their agreement with each of the items. If a subject places one of the two items in the first place (score '1'), the other item obviously can obtain only score '2'. This is also the case when the order of appearance of responses is taken into account.

Although it is outside the classic area of application of factor analysis, an ipsative data table can be factor-analyzed. However, special rules will govern its interpretation (Guilford, 1952). The following example illustrates the type of interpretation that can be made for such data structures in factor analysis.

Illustration: 'Who am I?'

We can have ipsative measurements when responses to an open question are thematically coded (content analysis). Some 600 pupils answered the question 'Who am I?' ten times in succession (Lorenzi-Cioldi and Meyer, 1984, pp. 48ff). Each of the ten answers was thematically coded in several categories. Two of them, consensual references (e.g., mention of group memberships and status. Example: 'I am a boy') and idiosyncratic references (e.g., personal qualities or flaws. Example: 'I am handsome'), were considered. Moreover, a number of pupils failed to complete the answers. For each pupil and each answer, we thus had three variables: two thematic categories and one possible non-answer. The coding in three categories was exclusive: for an individual, each answer was entered into only one of the two categories – consensual or idiosyncratic – or into the variable that represented the non-answer. A principal-component analysis (PCA) was performed for all of the vari-

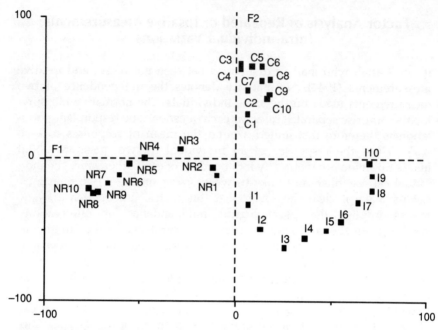

Figure 6.1   *Graphic representation of the contributions of variables on factors 1 and 2 of PCA on the responses to the question 'Who am I?'*

Note: (NR) stands for No responses, (C) for Consensual responses and (I) for Idiosyncratic responses. The number indicates the order of appearance of ten responses.

ables that described the ten answers to the question 'Who am I?' (PCA thus comprised a total of thirty variables). The first two dimensions accounted for 39 per cent and 13 per cent respectively of total variation. Figure 6.1 shows the space formed by the first two dimensions.

As shown in Figure 6.1, factor 1 concerned primarily subjects' progress from the first to the last response (or non-response). As they progressed in their self-definition, they tended to provide either idiosyncratic responses or no responses at all. It was found that consensual responses were poorly explained by this factor. This was to be related to numerous results already obtained from this test (see, for example, Kuhn and McPartland, 1955): subjects tended to respond by first providing 'sociological labels', social or collective positions ('I am a boy', etc.), and this tendency gradually subsided to make room for more abstract self-definitions in terms of tastes, personal references and existential values. Our results showed that the non-responses, located near the opposite pole of this dimension, constituted the alternative to the expression of this idiosyncrasy.

Dimension 2 opposed consensual responses to idiosyncratic responses and non-responses. This structure, which clarified the associations derived from the preceding dimension, indicated a sort of equiprobability of emergence, in each subject, of an idiosyncratic response or non-response after all consensual labels were exhausted. This dimension may be interpreted by using a decision process concerning the choice between responding in idiosyncratic terms or not responding.

As one can see, the notion of variation underlying factor analysis is interpreted differently, depending on specific questions asked in the research. First, this always involves covariations and, therefore, measurements of inter-profile relations. However, ipsative measurements would deal more directly with characteristics of the individual organization, while factor analysis usually prioritizes the organization of inter-individual differences.

Multidimensional Scaling or Factor Analysis?

The MDS approach to representations has been discussed in Part One. A number of critical differences separate MDS from factor analysis. The most important differences between these techniques with respect to SRs theory come from the type of data that are analyzed, their purposes, and the interpretation of the solutions. These differences must be taken into account when evaluating research needs.

MDS analyzes inter-stimulus similarities or differences and rests on the assumption of a homogeneous population. In the usual case, the inter-stimulus distances derive from the aggregation of the responses of a sample of individuals who judged similarities or differences between these stimuli. This matrix overrides the inter-individual variations in the sample. Accordingly, these similarities or differences could even be based on the responses of a single individual – a case that would be meaningless when using factor analysis. MDS is therefore a technique for stimulus-level examination.

Factor analysis, by contrast, is a technique for the examination of links between response profiles. At the most general level, this technique is much richer than MDS because it is capable of describing general links between responses in a population, as well as the individual differences. Specifically, it analyses inter-stimulus relationships derived from the responses of a sample of individuals. These relationships mirror inter-individual variations.

Major differences arise in the interpretation of the scaling and the factor solutions. The dimensions or the factors obtained result from the characteristics of these analytic methods. MDS is governed by the postulate that the dimensional space provides a geometrical representation of the perceptive space of subjects (in the case of aggregated data: an average, ideal or prototypical subject). Inter-stimulus distances are usually related to the concept of 'perceptual space' or of cognitive map, or even psychological schema. Of course, this postulate rests on the assumption that a metric method provides a model of the organization of the psychological space. In factor analysis, each dimension represents stimulus interrelations proceeding from a sample of individuals. But this stimulus space is only part of the solution. The inter-individual differences are at least as important. Factor scores for each dimension precisely indicate the position of each individual in relation to the common variation in the sample population to which he/she belongs. Factor scores are thus the measure of individual positioning in relation to a single concept, that is the 'label' that summarizes a pattern of loadings. There is no concept analogous to these individual scores in the MDS. The solution in this latter technique is that of a single individual or that of a hypothetical modal subject which represents the group as a whole. In MDS analyses, two dimensions are usually retained. These dimensions are then used to draw a space that in most cases is interpretable as a sort of photograph of the opinion. In factor analysis, factors can be interpreted as stands about which individuals take different positions – the more they differ one from another, the more variance the factor explains. This is a kind of information different from the one provided by the dimensions from the MDS.

As regards the study of SRs, whereas MDS receives a static interpretation of the inter-stimulus proximities and distances, that is, a sort of objectification of a representational field, factor analysis should be interpreted more dynamically in terms of heterogeneous but meaningful individual positions with respect to common reference points.

7

Multidimensional Scaling of Individual Differences:
Individual Distortions of a Mean Structure

The INDSCAL (individual differences multidimensional scaling, Carroll and Chang, 1970) model not only extends the characteristics of the MDS model (see Part One) but also goes beyond it on several major points. INDSCAL is very similar, but not identical, to factor analysis. Like the latter, INDSCAL aims at revealing a structure of individual differences or viewpoints against the background of shared reference points. It describes both a stimulus space and a person space. MDS analyzes a single matrix of distances or similarities. This matrix usually results from the mean of the responses of all the questioned subjects. Inter-individual differences or variations vanished in the computation of such a matrix. INDSCAL, by contrast, analyzes as many matrices of distances (or similarities) as there are individuals in the sample. Our reasoning about factor analysis, i.e., that it aims to describe inter-individual variations sparingly, may also apply to INDSCAL in that the latter aims at describing the variations between different distance matrices.

INDSCAL enables us first to describe a common mean space – a sort of compromise (cf. Coxon, 1982) between responses of various individuals – both conceptually and empirically similar to the space obtained by MDS. The novelty lies in the fact that each questioned individual is associated successively with weights that relate the common space to his/her 'private' space. The weight of an individual, when applied to the co-ordinates of the stimuli of the corresponding common dimension, deforms (stretches or shrinks, depending on the level of the weight) the group dimension. This distorted space fits better to the responses of a specific individual. The private spaces thus modify the overall picture of similarities provided by the common space (analogous to the stimulus space from the MDS) in order to make it fit better to the actual responses of particular individuals.

In INDSCAL, the weights are conceptually related to the scores calculated in factor analysis. A basic difference, however, is that a weight

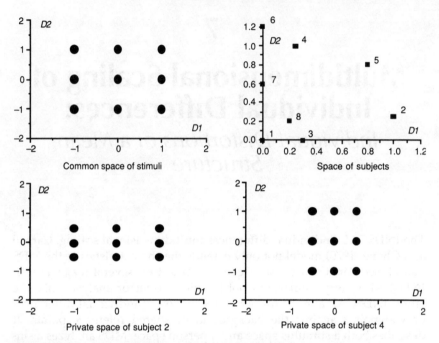

Figure 7.1   *Graphic representation of the common space of stimuli, of the space of subjects and of two private spaces of an illustrative example of MDS of individual differences*

Note: This illustration shows how one moves from the common space of stimuli to private spaces by using the weights of subjects on each dimension represented in the space of subjects. Figure adapted from Arabie, Carroll and DeSarbo, 1987, 20.

does not indicate any position on the common dimension. All individuals are assumed to share this space, but the weight indicates the *salience* or the *importance* of this dimension for the individual. In other words, the weight indicates the extent to which an individual uses this dimension in his/her judgements. For this reason, the weights generally have only a positive value.

In summary, the common and the private spaces are the two basic notions of INDSCAL (see Figure 7.1). The common space is the stimulus configuration in a multidimensional space (the number of dimensions is determined similarly to MDS). It is therefore a reference or theoretical space, a compromise between the spaces of all individuals and to which their private spaces conform with degrees that can be quantified. The common space therefore does not necessarily describe the responses of any subject in particular. As in factor analysis, dimensions are presented in an order reflecting the decreasing amount of explained variation. The meaning of the word 'variation' and its particularity with respect to its equivalent in factor analysis will be clarified in the examples below (see Figure 7.1).

These examples show the usefulness of INDSCAL for the study of SRs. One of the aims pursued through these examples is to clarify the relationship between common and private spaces in order to determine precisely the contribution of this model compared with factor analysis. We will then discuss different ways of treating the weights of individuals and their private spaces. The last and more complex example will illustrate a few variants of the use of INDSCAL to show specific modalities of variations in responses.

Multidimensional Scaling of a Word Classification Task

Common Space

To make the illustration as clear as possible, we will now give a fictitious numerical example concerning one procedure – free classification of objects – widely used in the study of SRs. Let us imagine asking subjects freely to assort six objects representing cognitive activities according to their similarities or differences. These objects are, for example, *thinking*, *informing oneself*, *deciding*, *organizing*, *dreaming* and *imagining*. Let us also assume that subjects can form as many categories as they wish (at least one category composed of the six objects and at most six categories with one object in each).

Table 7.1 shows the responses of six individuals. Each of them is represented by a similarity matrix (co-occurrence matrices in this case). These matrices are symmetrical, of course, because they comprise the six objects in row and in column. At the intersection of a row and a column, we have entered '0' if the two corresponding objects have not been placed in the same group and '1' if these objects have been placed together in the same group. One notices that the diagonal of each matrix has only '1': the similarity of each cognitive activity to itself is obviously maximal.

The classic treatment of such responses was MDS or HCA of the matrix aggregating the individual matrices shown in Table 7.1. These two procedures yielded very similar results. Let us consider the example of MDS.

As we will see with INDSCAL, this two-dimensional space corresponds fairly closely to the space of the first two dimensions obtained by analyzing individual differences. With this type of data matrix, however, it is impossible directly to test the salience of dimensions for each individual, i.e. for each response configuration.

Table 7.1   *Responses of six individuals selecting six cognitive activities (fictitious example).*

	Individual responses

Matrices of individual co-occurrences									

	Th	Io	De	Or	Dr	Im			
Th	1								
Io	1	1							
De	0	0	1				Individual 1		
Or	0	0	1	1			response: (ThIo)	(DeOr)	(DrIm)
Dr	0	0	0	0	1				
Im	0	0	0	0	1	1			

	Th	Io	De	Or	Dr	Im		
Th	1							
Io	1	1						
De	1	1	1				Individual 2	
Or	0	0	0	1			response: (ThIoDe)	(OrDrIm)
Dr	0	0	0	1	1			
Im	0	0	0	1	1	1		

	Th	Io	De	Or	Dr	Im			
Th	1								
Io	0	1							
De	0	0	1				Individual 3		
Or	1	0	0	1			response: (ThOr)	(IoDr)	(DeIm)
Dr	0	1	0	0	1				
Im	0	0	1	0	0	1			

	Th	Io	De	Or	Dr	Im			
Th	1								
Io	1	1							
De	1	1	1				Individual 4		
Or	0	0	0	1			response: (ThIoDe)	(Dr)	(OrIm)
Dr	0	0	0	0	1				
Im	0	0	0	1	0	1			

	Th	Io	De	Or	Dr	Im			
Th	1								
Io	0	1							
De	0	1	1				Individual 5		
Or	1	0	0	1			response: (ThOr)	(IoDe)	(DrIm)
Dr	0	0	0	0	1				
Im	0	0	0	0	1	1			

	Th	Io	De	Or	Dr	Im			
Th	1								
Io	1	1							
De	1	1	1				Individual 6		
Or	0	0	0	1			response: (ThIoDe)	(Or)	(DrIm)
Dr	0	0	0	0	1				
Tm	0	0	0	0	1	1			

Note: (Th) thinking, (Io) informing oneself,
    (De) deciding, (Or) organizing, (Dr) dreaming
    and (Im) imagining
On the right are the classifications of six stimuli operated by each subject. On the left is the retranscription of these responses in similarity matrices (matrices of individual co-occurrences)

Table 7.2 *MDS results and table of analyzed data. Coordinates of stimuli in the two-dimensional space*

| | Dimension | | Aggregated data | | | | | |
	1	2	Th	Io	De	Or	Dr	Im
Object								
Thinking	1.08	–0.03	6					
Informing oneself	1.12	0.44	4	6				
Deciding	1.12	0.44	3	4	6			
Organizing	–0.36	–1.71	2	0	1	6		
Dreaming	–1.47	0.65	0	1	0	1	6	
Imagining	–1.49	0.20	0	0	1	2	4	6

Note: Stress: 0.047

Individual Distortions

INDSCAL first measures overall stress (0.13) and stresses for each of the six matrices entered (one sees immediately that this method explains matrix 1 least well and matrices 2 and 3 best, as shown by Table 7.3).

We then obtain the actual INDSCAL results, the co-ordinates of the six objects on three dimensions (see Table 7.4; three dimensions are chosen according to criteria that will be clarified later). Thus, we first have

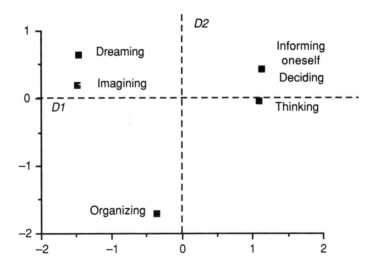

Figure 7.2 *Graphic representation of dimensions 1 and 2 of MDS on cognitive activities.*

Table 7.3   *Results of INDSCAL of individual responses shown in Table 7.1. Stresses associated with individual matrices for three dimensions*

Individual	Stress
1	0.17
2	0.09
3	0.05
4	0.15
5	0.14
6	0.14
overall	0.13

the common space of all our subjects.

Let us now interpret the results of this analysis. Dimension 1 isolates *thinking, informing oneself* and *deciding* on the one hand and the remaining cognitive activities on the other. An examination of individual weights (Table 7.4) shows that it is individual 2 (weight = 0.99) who uses this dimension most. By reverting to the initial responses, we verify that this is indeed the grouping carried out by this individual. Individuals 4 and 6 also use this dimension to a lesser extent, however. Both individuals have carried out similar but not identical groupings: they have grouped the objects *thinking, informing oneself* and *deciding*, but do not agree on the first dimension that restores the grouping of the objects *organizing, dreaming* and *imagining* in two different ways that will affect their respective weights. Individual 6 isolates the object *organizing*, which gives him/her the appreciable weight of 0.67. But individual 4, who nonetheless also makes three groups of objects, contradicts this dimension further by making the grouping *dreaming* versus *organizing* and *imagining*, which gives him/her the slightly lower weight of 0.50.

Let us now consider an individual who has appreciably higher

Table 7.4   *Results of INDSCAL of individual responses shown in Table 7.1. Common space and weights of individuals on three dimensions*

Dimension:	Common space Co-ordinates of objects				Space of individuals Weights of individuals		
	1	2	3		1	2	3
Object				Individual			
Thinking	−0.92	−1.30	0.28	1	0.06	0.05	0.05
Informing self	−1.04	0.71	1.12	2	0.99	0.05	0.00
Deciding	−1.04	0.47	−1.31	3	0.06	0.69	0.71
Organizing	0.92	−1.49	0.06	4	0.50	0.28	0.27
Dreaming	1.02	0.96	1.14	5	0.40	0.42	0.25
Imagining	1.05	0.66	−1.29	6	0.67	0.39	0.19

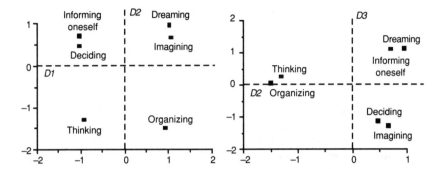

Figure 7.3   *Graphic representation of the common space of INDSCAL on cognitive activities: dimensions 1 and 2 (on the left) and dimensions 2 and 3 (on the right).*

weights on two dimensions. Individual 3 has high weights on dimensions 2 and 3. One first notices that, if an individual has high weights on two dimensions, this justifies reading a space that intersects the two corresponding dimensions. One then observes that the space of Figure 7.3 faithfully restores the classification carried out by this individual in terms of the objects *thinking* and *organizing, informing oneself* and *dreaming*, and *deciding* and *imagining*.

One finally observes that the common space cannot adequately reproduce local variations in responses. This is true of individual 1, who has very low weights on three dimensions and is therefore not well represented by INDSCAL. In fact, part of his/her groupings is well represented by dimension 1 (objects *thinking* and *informing oneself* versus objects *dreaming* and *imagining*). However, since this individual has also carried out the grouping of the objects *deciding* and *organizing*, which is poorly represented in this dimension, he/she will have a low weight.

The oppositions and complementarities between INDSCAL and factor analysis begin to appear. Dimension 1 of our INDSCAL, for example, opposes the objects *thinking, informing oneself* and *deciding* to the objects *organizing, dreaming* and *imagining*. This opposition reflects the most frequent grouping in the population. A high individual weight on this dimension does not, of course, signify the 'position' of an individual on the continuum (reasoning that would be characteristic of factor analysis). The individual carrying out such a grouping should not be placed near either pole of this dimension. He/she achieves the entire dimension signifying the given grouping. The weight thus does indicate the extent to which a given individual uses this dimension or its salience.

Multidimensional Scaling and Interpretation
of Individual Variations

Illustration: the Occupational Field

Lorenzi-Cioldi and Joye (1988) proposed an SR collection technique based on the free classification of stimuli. Such a classification not only extends the usefulness of this technique but also makes respondents' task easier and simpler. The authors started with the idea that most classic approaches, which use a set of items on which subjects place occupations (normative measurements), force them to ponder the interoccupational relations according to (a) common, (b) unidimensional and bipolar, and (c) linear criteria. We also know that the ceiling, halo and social-desirability effects usually appear when scales are used. To avoid these pitfalls, the authors instructed the subjects (ninety-four men and eighty-seven women, a quota sample of the French-speaking Swiss population) to freely place eighteen occupations on a square surface. These occupations had been pre-selected according to three criteria: sex connotation, prestige and degree of independence. The instructions given orally by the investigator were the following:

> Some occupations are similar, while others are different. There are many ways of considering them similar or different, i.e. many ways of grouping or differentiating them. We will give you a list of occupations. Each one of them is written on a piece of cardboard. Please arrange these pieces on the square by putting together the occupations that seem to you the most similar and putting away those that seem to you the most different. Of course, you may use all the places of the square.

To evaluate the configuration established by subjects, each of them received, once the task was completed, two additional pieces of paper bearing the legend 'the most desirable' and 'the least desirable' and also designed to be placed on the square surface. Subjects then estimated the average monthly pay of each occupation (the pay criterion, usually used to classify occupations, was proposed to check the dimensions obtained).

The main advantage of this procedure is to enable subjects to formulate their responses in a space which, unlike the standard space of scales, does not induce pre-orientation. Standard analysis of responses on scales by factor analysis is, however, no longer possible or even desirable. The main significance of this approach lies, in fact, in distances between stimuli – occupations – more than in terms of their correlations.

For each respondent, one can calculate a matrix comprising all the distances between the eighteen occupations. According to the prerequisites of INDSCAL, one thus has as many distance matrices as subjects. In our example (Lorenzi-Cioldi and Joye, 1988), INDSCAL provided four common dimensions (see Table 7.5) identified as follows: status in the conventional sense of the word, occupational independence, occupational practice indoors or outdoors and sex connotation (these dimensions are identified similarly to factor analysis). The weights of individuals are, moreover, associated with each dimension.

The estimated pay of the above-listed occupations – the 'objective' criterion – turned out to be correlated with the first dimension (status: $r = 0.70$). This coefficient, though high, did not reach a value permitting full explanation for the structure (49 per cent of variance shared by status and pay). This does indicate that a hierarchy of occupations based on their relative status is actually built according to a combination of more complex criteria.

The quota sample of the study population was thus composed of several subgroups of subjects: men and women in different socioprofessional categories and of different educational backgrounds. One can therefore use the weights of subjects (spaces of subjects) as new dependent variables to subject them to analyses designed to describe the differences between subgroups of individuals. However, one can also calcu-

Table 7.5   *INDSCAL results for the occupational field: positions of occupations on four common dimensions*

	Dimension			
	1	2	3	4
Occupation				
Female packer	1.48	1.02	0.21	−0.58
Saleswoman	1.36	0.94	0.50	−0.56
Deliveryman	1.34	0.99	0.41	0.47
Bus driver	1.14	0.66	0.41	0.91
Farm worker	0.94	−0.06	−1.66	1.04
Female potter	0.70	−1.31	−0.03	−1.56
Seamstress	0.55	−1.38	−0.01	−1.47
Bookbinder	0.42	−1.47	−0.14	−1.54
Mason	0.35	−0.95	−1.27	0.71
Peasant	−0.07	−1.04	−2.04	0.88
Employee	−0.67	1.49	−0.45	-0.77
Foreman	−0.76	0.47	−0.74	1.09
Teacher	−0.82	0.34	1.02	−1.16
Executive secretary	−1.13	1.18	−0.20	−0.80
Insurance agent	−1.15	1.21	−0.08	0.54
Small-business owner	−1.17	−0.69	0.41	1.36
Female lawyer	−1.25	−0.64	1.85	0.69
Doctor	−1.26	−0.75	1.83	0.76

late Pearson correlations between weights (overall or per subgroup) to test the co-occurrence of dimensions (a salary dimension can thus be varyingly correlated with a sex dimension or the latter can also be correlated with a dimension of occupational independence). The following remarks serve only to illustrate the possible ways of treating individual weights.

One can first set a minimum threshold above which a dimension is considered to have been adopted by a given individual and below which it is considered not to have been adopted. It is actually a matter of dichotomizing the weight continuum. For each dimension, for example, the threshold can be so chosen that 25 per cent of individuals are found in the 'adoption' category and the remaining 75 per cent in the 'non-adoption' category. For each dimension, there is thus one type available. By intersecting these types two by two, it became apparent that the independence dimension was significantly correlated with the dimension opposing the male to the female. In other words, the subjects who used the independence dimension also used the sex dimension. This latter dimension, moreover, did not seem directly to denote status differences in the occupations, but rather their practice in a context of independence or subordination. The variations in individual weights on a given dimension could then be related to variables external to the analysis, such as respondents' sex, occupation and educational level. It then became apparent, for instance, that respondents with the lowest educational levels and the least prestigious occupations adopted the dimensions of status and sex connotation to a larger extent.

In the end, one realized that individuals structured the occupational universe according to a limited number of shared dimensions, but that there were considerable differences in the degree of importance different individuals attached to different dimensions. Moreover, several dimensions, i.e., criteria for classifying occupations, were used concomitantly by most subjects. INDSCAL thus showed that starting with an 'inventory' of classification criteria common to a given population (provided by the common space of INDSCAL), the perception of social hierarchies tended to become blurred as respondents' status rose.

Illustration: Similarities Between Nations

INDSCAL was used by Wish, Deutsch and Biener (1970) in their research on the organization of representations of various nations. In a first investigation conducted in April 1968, eighteen psychology students indicated on a nine-point scale the degree of similarity they perceived between nations for each of the sixty-six possible pairs of a total of twelve nations. This task completed, the same subjects answered questions about their opinions on the Vietnam War. The subjects were classified as 'doves', 'moderates' or 'hawks', depending on whether they favoured withdrawing American troops from Vietnam, making concessions to the enemy or further stepping up the US war effort. The two most important dimensions of the similarities between nations detected by INDSCAL can be described as follows.

The first dimension referred to 'political and ideological alignment'. The nations aligned with the Soviet Union or the People's Republic of China were grouped together and opposed to those more aligned with the United States. The neutral or non-aligned nations had intermediate values on this dimension. Considering that the most developed nations were projected higher than the others on the second dimension, this latter was interpreted as concerning 'economic development'. A third dimension was less easy to interpret. It was worded 'geography and culture', however, in view of the fact that it roughly separated the Western from the Eastern nations. Of course geography and culture are closely linked in the real world, and it is therefore difficult to separate them in the interpretation of dimensions.

Subjects' weights on the first two dimensions showed, first, that all hawks were projected higher on the first dimension than on the second. This fact indicated that political alignment was a factor more important than economic development in their ratings of similarity between nations. The relative and absolute weight for economic development was higher for doves than for hawks. Moreover, these attitudinal subgroups did not differ systematically in their weighting of the third dimension.

While political alignment was only slightly more important for hawks than for doves, economic development was clearly more salient for doves than for hawks. In fact, four out of six hawks virtually disregarded economic development in their assessments of similarity between nations. These results suggest that hawks were more swayed than doves by evaluative considerations of a political nature.

In a second investigation, the list was expanded to include twenty-one nations. There were more subjects ($N = 75$), and they were Columbia University undergraduates from different countries. As in the first survey, they rated the degree of similarity between different countries and responded to various other scales for each country. The first two dimensions again concerned political alignment and economic development. The significance of the additional scales lay in the fact that they enabled the description of countries on different scales to be related to their positions on the INDSCAL dimensions.

Let us analyze this relationship for the first two dimensions. The political-alignment dimension was more closely correlated with the descriptions on each scale for hawks than for doves. This was especially true for scales of a highly evaluative nature such as 'I love', 'Good' and 'Looks like an ideal country', while the differences were smaller for more objective characteristics such as 'Big', 'Rich' and 'Powerful'. In their descriptions on a wide variety of scales, the 'non-doves' were thus apparently more influenced than the doves by the political-alignment aspect of the countries rated.

While accounting for only a small part of the analyses, these results show that it may be interesting to combine different investigative techniques. A comparison of descriptions on scales and dimensions obtained by INDSCAL illustrates the significance of organizing principles at work in the SRs of countries. Moreover, the difference between correlations for two subgroups of subjects shows that the same organizing principle intervenes differently according to certain political affinities.

Multidimensional Scaling and Differences Between Respondents and Between Responses

Illustration: Social Relationships

Wish *et al.* (Wish, 1976; Wish, Deutsch and Kaplan, 1976) studied the SRs of twenty-five social relationships (e.g. between husband and wife, between prison guard and inmate, between two enemies and between two political opponents). The main aim of this study was to describe the dimensions underlying the conceptions of these different social relationships. Subjects answered several questions asking them to rate social relationships in general (called prototypical relationships) and in terms of their own personal history (specific relationships). We will summarize this research to show how various data-analysis techniques complement each other in the study of the organization and variation of representations.

Ratings of Prototypical Relationships

Eighty-seven subjects (men) performed three different tasks:

1 They directly rated the similarity between each pair of social relationships (300 ratings) on scales ranging from 1 (completely similar) to 9 (completely different). These ratings enabled the researchers to obtain directly a matrix of proximities between social relationships (twenty-five rows and twenty-five columns) for each subject.
2 They freely provided five to ten characteristics shared by at least two social relationships (by indicating the social relationships to which

each characteristic provided applies). The proximity matrix for each subject was then defined as follows: the degree of similarity between two given social relationships is the number of times a subject also applies a characteristic common to these two relationships (minimum = 0; maximum = 10).

3 They rated the social relationships on twenty-five bipolar nine-point scales. These scales represented the most relevant evaluative and descriptive aspects (examples: *tense–relaxed, compatible–incompatible goals, co-operative–competitive, interesting–boring, flexible–rigid, intense–superficial* and *similar–different*). In view of the large number of possible ratings, each subject actually used only fourteen out of a total of twenty-five scales. The rating matrix therefore mixed the information collected from different subjects. The final distances between the twenty-five relationships aggregated the responses to the fourteen scales of each subject (the scales were thus confounded in statistical analysis). The coefficients thus calculated gave the overall distances between social relationships for all of the scales.

One thus sees that the data used for analysis were heterogeneous in nature.

Using the bipolar-scale technique described above, subjects also rated a subset of twenty social relationships in which they themselves were involved. Certain relationships plunged the subject into his childhood (e.g., 'between you and your parents'), while other relationships did the same with regard to the present ('between you and your children').

Representations of Social Relationships

Three different INDSCAL analyses (one for each collection method) were first performed for prototypical relationships. In each analysis, the different proximity matrices represented respectively the distances between the twenty-five social relationships for each individual. Four dimensions were chosen in each analysis. To measure the differences between response structures by different collection techniques, Wish, Deutsch and Kaplan (1976) compared the dimensions obtained by each of the methods. To do so, they calculated correlations between the co-ordinates of the dimensions obtained by separate analyses. These correlations turned out to be high, which led them to conclude that the stability of representations did not depend on the collection method used. This stability also appeared when the correlations between the individual weights of each analysis were calculated.

In view of the high value of the correlations, the authors reduced their results to a single space. For each dimension, they calculated the mean of the co-ordinates of the three analyses. Of course, new correlations between each dimension of this mean space and the co-ordinates of each dimension of the three initial analyses were very high again. These results now justified aggregating different methods of collecting representations.

The four dimensions were then interpreted according to an external criterion by multiple regression analysis (MRA). The common space described the proximities between the twenty-five social relationships. The authors then used as dependent variables the mean ratings of each bipolar scale of the semantic differential (task 3). The mean ratings of the twenty-five social relationships on a bipolar scale thus resulted in as many MRAs (twenty-five analyses or one for each bipolar scale), including the series of co-ordinates of the social relationships on the four dimensions as independent variables.

Here is therefore the finally proposed interpretation of each of the four dimensions obtained according to the Beta coefficients of regression. The interpretation was based on the bipolar scales that were closely correlated with the co-ordinates of the dimensions. The typical relationships that emerged on each dimension illustrated, moreover, the content of the dimension. Dimension 1: the bipolar scale that had the closest correlation with the co-ordinates of the social relationships was competitive versus co-operative. Examples of social relationships present on this dimension were: divorced couple, personal enemies, political opponents versus good friends, husband–wife, and team mates. Dimension 2: unequal versus equal (examples: prison guard–inmate, interviewer–interviewee, teacher–pupil, parent–child versus team mates, political opponents, good friends, personal enemies and cousins). Dimension 3: socio–emotional–oriented towards task completion (examples: parent–child, brother–sister, husband–wife versus interviewer–job applicant, seller–buyer and political opponents). Dimension 4: intense-superficial (examples: parent–child, husband–wife, good friends, psychotherapist–patient versus chance encounters, interviewer–interviewee and employee–employer).

After interpreting the dimensions, the authors studied individual differences. Analyses of variance were performed by taking individual weights for each dimension as dependent variables. It is unimportant for us here to discuss in detail the differences thus obtained (it was found, for instance, that dimension 1 *competitive versus co-operative* was used more by those aged over twenty-five and that dimension 2 *unequal versus equal* was used more by left-wing sympathizers). Of significance is the fact that in individual differences in the use of the common and consensual space were thus taken into account and described.

Using the semantic differential, subjects also rated twenty specific social relationships, i.e. relationships in which they were or had been involved. Their responses made it possible to set up distance matrices comparing prototypical and specific relationships. The matrices were of 45×45 type (twenty-five typical social relationships and twenty specific social relationships for each bipolar scale and not for each subject here). One thus had twenty-five matrices or one matrix for each bipolar scale used. The novelty of this approach must be emphasized: the weights obtained by INDSCAL will concern each bipolar scale and not each individual.

In this case, it is quite natural to begin interpreting the dimensions by examining the weights of bipolar scales. This will make it easier to interpret dimensions themselves. Thus, for example, one had a high weight on dimension 1 for the scale *co-operative–competitive* and on dimension 2 for the scales *equal–unequal, similar–different roles* and *democratic–autocratic*. A high weight of a bipolar scale on a dimension indicated the importance of this bipolar scale for the interpretation of dimensions. The second dimension was therefore interpreted as being related to the symmetry of social relationships.

One then understands how the authors were able to interpret the dimensions comprising forty-five (25+20) social relationships even before examining the co-ordinates of these forty-five stimuli. The social relationships will now be distributed on a space that already has a meaning. Thus, for example, the 'symmetry' dimension indicates power distribution between two individuals involved in the relationship. If the co-ordinate of a social relationship is different from zero on this dimension, the *symmetrical* versus *asymmetrical* opposition can be held responsible for this difference. Thus, for example, subjects thought of their childhood relationship with their parents as less co-operative (dimension 1) and less egalitarian than their current relationship with their own children.

The results show that typical relationships are placed at the extremities of the axes, while specific relationships are more attracted towards the centre. Subjects idealized or extremized prototypical relationships compared with their specific relationships, as evidenced by the fact that more variations were observed in the co-ordinates of typical relationships than in the co-ordinates of specific relationships on the same dimension. The variations between typical relationships were greater than the corresponding variations in specific relationships. In other words, the differences between typical relationships, in terms of bipolar dimensions, were more clearly perceived by subjects than the differences between specific relationships in which they were involved.

On the other hand, by considering raw responses on these same bipolar scales, the authors observed more inter-individual variations in the ratings of specific relationships than in others. This was demonstrated by a simple calculation of the variance for each of the relationships (variances for the twenty-five bipolar scales for each relationship and each subject).

Since INDSCAL operates on variations between different matrices, it may be surprising that its results place specific relationships (where there are more inter-individual variations) near the centre of the space and typical relationships at the periphery. This is, however, simply due to the fact that the observation units of the analyzed matrices were not individuals, but bipolar scales. In fact, bipolar scales do distinguish between typical relationships, and individuals differ from each other much more in specific relationships, but on each of the scales.

When Wish, Deutsch and Kaplan (1976) conducted two more IND-SCAL analyses, one for specific relationships and the other for typical relationships with the individual as a unit, and when they ran an analysis of variance on the weights of each of the analyses (independent factors: sex, for instance), they found, in fact, a larger number of significant differences between the weights of subgroups of subjects for specific relationships than for typical relationships.

From Consensus to Individual Positioning

The idea of shared knowledge is now described in at least two different ways. First, from consensus or an inter-individual agreement shown by the similarity of responses, one moves on to the sharing of reference points and to individual positioning. This positioning implies multiplicity, diversity and opposition both conceptually and statistically. Then, the idea of a single or unidimensional score of consensus is replaced by the idea of a plurality of dimensions (or individual positions) that are relatively independent of each other. Depending on the technique used, the examples have shown that individual variations can be organized (factor analysis) or that subjects attach more or less importance to these variations (INDSCAL).

While individuals have been described by their differences, these have not been treated for what they owe to the multiple social insertions of individuals, to interactional situations, etc. Such an examination should show the coherence of various positions and of types of individual differences. Thus, while factor analysis presupposes homogeneous populations, INDSCAL cannot tolerate that individuals differ from each other too systematically for fear of witnessing the emergence of a common space too different from individual spaces and thus artificial and difficult to interpret.

It is, however, inter-individual variations that have, thanks to factor analysis, revealed the organizing principles of individual positions in relation to issues that are considered important for the members of a given population. And it is also inter-individual variations that have, through INDSCAL, permitted describing the individual modulations of a 'common map', i.e., the modulations of a representational field considered to be shared.

In Part Three, we will look at another (complementary) aspect of the study of inter-individual differences that are organized explicitly according to individuals' group memberships and social positions. The techniques used, and notably certain CFA models, have been designed to reveal such contrasts.

PART III

Group Effects on Individual Positioning

In Parts One and Two, we have first seen how researchers endeavoured to define representational fields, since SRs are considered to be collective realities that are, in a way, independent of individual variations. The aim of their endeavour was to bring together the views of several individuals on an aspect of their social environment in a single 'objective' reality. The primary concern of these researchers was to draw up a sort of objective map of SRs. We have then shown how SRs have been studied as principles organizing inter-individual differences. From this viewpoint, main analytic techniques were used to define and measure individual positions in representational fields. We are now interested to find out what happens when social actors collectively take a definite position on these scenes as groups defining themselves in relation to each other. Does the representational field change when appropriate techniques are used to locate the social actors there by taking their social memberships and positions into account?

Some researchers remain firmly attached to the idea that the representational field is a single reality in which groups, however, can occupy different positions. From their viewpoint, analytic methods should account for differences in positions of individuals according to their membership in social groups or categories. These differences in positions may be assessed with various techniques. Some approaches are characterized by the fact that describing different positions is a 'post-event' operation – a sort of weighting applied to a shared multidimensional structure. In a certain sense, authors in this tradition consider that common SRs intervene very forcefully in shaping individual representations to such an extent that different group memberships or specific social experiences allow for variations only in the degree to which individuals adhere to shared representations.

Other researchers, by contrast, try to build representational fields such that groups of individuals become differentiated from each other as much as possible. Notably, the SRs described by these authors have specific reality only in so far as they allow social groups to occupy different positions. Authors adopting such approaches are more interested in assessing the originality of representations held by various groups than in defining what they have in common.

We will consider following techniques that often convey a holistic conception of SR: use of supplementary variables in CFA, determination of the centres of gravity of groups, automatic interaction detection. The last two chapters will deal with data-analysis methods that were more directly used to study social change and differentiation, namely discriminant analysis and a method for textual-data correspondence analysis.

The meaning of an SR cannot be exhaustively studied without analyzing its relationships with a more general system of symbolic relationships. SRs are more than general beliefs or organizing principles of individual differences as they receive their specificity from their anchoring in social systems of symbolic relationships.

Anchoring of social SRs has mainly been studied in three different ways. First, the relationships with general beliefs and values (such as belief in a just world or egalitarianism) have been investigated. Such values and beliefs are considered general to the extent that they supposedly organize symbolic relationships in various domains. SRs have also been studied as anchored in the views individuals develop on the structuring of their social environment, as for instance the representations they hold concerning relationships between social groups and categories. Finally, a third way of analyzing the anchoring of SRs investigates how group memberships or social positions held by individuals influence their SRs, the general hypothesis being that shared social insertions lead to specific interactions and experiences that modulate SRs.

The first and second kind of studies analyze to a certain extent relationships between contents or organizing principles of different SRs. An example of the first kind of analysis has been developed in Chapter 6 when explanations of particular delinquent acts were studied as a function of individuals' adherence to general beliefs about causes and treatments of delinquency. In the previous chapter, we cited the study of Wish, Deutsch and Kaplan (1976) and their analysis of the links between descriptions of prototypical and specific social relationships which is an illustration of the second way of studying the anchoring of SRs.

The third kind of studies compares SRs of groups or categories of individuals as a function of the positions they occupy in a network of social relations. Methodologically these studies aim to assess differences and they use appropriate techniques which will be presented in this Part as they differ from the ones described in the previous parts.

8

Correspondence Analysis and Study of Anchoring

Correspondence Analysis of Frequency Tables: Social Variations in Responses

The primary function of correspondence analysis is to treat, as already shown above, tables of frequency data. In this case, the technique is called simple or statistical correspondence analysis. One may imagine that the frequency of responses to questionnaire items is crossed with respondents' membership in groups defined by their social status. Reading such a data table provides information on the relations between individuals' group membership and their responses to a given question. Correspondence analysis can be used to analyze the rows and columns of such a table. It is particularly useful when its dimensions and the complexity of relations make its content difficult to understand. In this case, this technique not only detects a link between various SR components but also sheds light on the relationship between these representational components and individuals' integration into groups, for example of different social status.

We will now consider an example of statistical correspondence analysis and then examine the extension of this technique to so-called multiple correspondence analysis.

Illustration: Social Status and Intelligence

A table taken from a survey conducted in 1911 in London on the representations of pupils by their teachers will serve as an example for describing the technique (see Cibois, 1984, 13–18). The pupils were divided into six groups according to their scholastic performance (very talented, remarkable, fairly intelligent, slow but intelligent, slow, and slow and stupid). The same teachers also rated the social status of each pupil separately. The indicator used at the time was the way the pupils were dressed and was divided into four categories (very well dressed, well dressed, poorly but passably dressed and insufficiently dressed). At the intersection of a row and a column, the frequency table indicated the number of pupils who had a given scholastic performance level and a given social status (type of dress). Ratings of intelligence and social status were called sets of modalities. One may then wonder if there was a relationship between the two series of measurements and what type of relationship was at work while assessing its closeness. It was therefore necessary to find out if the representations of pupils in terms of intelligence levels had links with their social status (individuals' membership in groups defined by the way they were dressed).

The classic response to such questions is to compare frequencies in the table's margins with frequencies in its squares – frequencies resulting from the intersection of the table's rows and columns. This reasoning leads to the calculation of 'deviations from independence' in each square of the table, since the independence criterion is met when it is found that the proportions within the table correspond to the products of the proportions in the margins. A Chi-square value, thus calculated, will enable us to decide whether to reject or accept the hypothesis of absence of relationship between the two series of measurements.

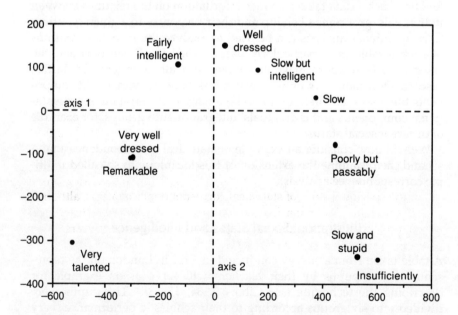

Figure 8.1   *Graphic representation of modalities on the first two factor axes of CFA on the relationship between social status and intelligence.*

Note: According to Gilby's survey (London, 1911) reported by Cibois, 1984, 14.

Correspondence analysis permits an alternate and complementary examination of this table and represents the rows and columns of the data table (groups of social status and intelligence levels) simultaneously. The graphs drawn using factors or dimensions represent, in a common space, the conjunction of intelligence levels and social positions. Figure 8.1 shows the results of correspondence analysis of the frequency table presented by Cibois (1984, 14).

The two factors account for 78 per cent and 20 per cent respectively of the deviations from independence in the table. The analysis therefore summarizes nearly all of the information contained therein. Let us first consider factor 1, which is the most important in view of the amount of explained deviation. The results are read using the contributions available for each set of modalities, rows and columns (see Chapter 3 in this connection). The graph shows that the modalities of social status are arranged from left to right according to their level: the highest statuses (e.g. very well dressed) are thus the opposite of the other statuses (e.g. insufficiently dressed). In the same space, intelligence ratings are superposed onto this distribution of social statuses. One thus sees that the most favourable modalities (e.g. very talented) are also located on the left and are the opposite of the least favourable modalities (e.g. slow and stupid).

Of great interest is also the distribution of the modalities on factor 2. In fact, this factor opposes the intermediate modalities of memberships and intelligence ratings (e.g. well dressed and fairly intelligent) to all the extreme modalities of the table. The intersection of the two factors, the first opposing the extremes of hierarchy and the second opposing the mean categories to the extremes, then shows a parabolic cloud. This characteristic shape, which appears whenever a close link emerges between the modalities of one and the other set of the table, is called the 'Guttman effect' (see Lorenzi-Cioldi, 1983, 370–3; English-speaking researchers use the evocative expression 'horseshoe'. See, for example, Coxon and Davies, 1986, 114ff).

The approach that consists of building a single factor space according to the links between two or more groups (SRs and membership groups) is not the specific feature of statistical correspondence analysis, although this method may be regarded as a prototypical technique. Canonical correlation analysis and discriminant analysis in particular are other examples that will be discussed later in this chapter.

Passive Variables in Correspondence Analysis: Social and Field Characteristics

The logic forming the basis of statistical correspondence analysis, which usually has no passive elements, has been extended to permit the analysis of a vast range of data tables that are not all structured like contingency tables (see Chapter 3; for an illustration of the diversity of tables analyzable by this technique, see Fénelon, 1981). This is the so-called multiple correspondence analysis (MCA). MCA analyzes a data matrix intersecting a set of modalities (representational elements) and individuals. The social memberships of these individuals are entered later into the analysis as passive variables. This procedure is similar to a method that consists of performing a principal-component analysis (PCA) of these same data, then calculating individual positions on factors (factor scores) and analyzing the variations in these positions according to variables external to the analysis by means of analysis of variance or hierarchical cluster analysis (HCA) (see below).

The rules for interpreting the MCA results and in particular the rules for graph reading differ nonetheless on an important point from the rules for interpreting the statistical correspondence analysis results. This difference arises from the presence of passive modalities that have a different theoretical and statistical status. In fact, passive elements (social positions) are placed by MCA at the centre of the subset of active modalities (representations) to which they are closest. The relations of the passive modalities between themselves, however, must be ignored because these modalities did not participate in axis construction.

This approach is undoubtedly most useful for studying SRs. The membership groups of respondents are projected into the space of responses and thus, in a way, of representations. The significance of such an approach was described with great clarity by Cibois (1984, 130–1):

> Another typical example consists of opposing the universe of opinion variables to that of status variables (also conventionally called 'explanatory' variables) such as sex, age and socioprofessional category. Experience has shown that, if all these questions are put into active variables, it becomes very difficult to distinguish the links between opinion variables from those between status variables. To get a clearer picture of all this, only questions about opinions are put into active variables, while status variables are put into passive variables. One thus has an opinion configuration without interference from the links between status variables. On the other hand, the status variables come to place themselves closest to the opinion modalities that are most similar to them (i.e., most frequently chosen by the same individuals). If there was independence between opinion variables and status variables, all passive opinion modalities would come to place themselves at the centre of the graph. If there was a very close link between certain opinion and status modalities, however,

there would be a very close conjunction that would tend to super-pose if the same individuals took the two modalities together. Most of the time, one finds oneself in an intermediate situation: there is a link between opinion variables and status variables, but it is far less close than between opinion variables, for example.

In sociology, Bourdieu (1979, 293–301) was one of the first to use this technique, for example for visualizing the relationship between different sociocultural variables and taste structures of the dominant social classes. Let us, however, make a critical observation with regard to the analyses performed by Bourdieu. Obviously, sociologists do not analyze the taste field as an autonomous structure independent of the socioeconomic and cultural insertion and position modalities. In this, they take an approach opposite to that of most psychologists. But they adhere to their conception of recognition/lack of recognition according to which the apparent autonomy of an easily 'recognizable' field actually expresses individual positions that have (often 'unrecognized') homologous links with integration into the field of economic and cultural power.

The social positions usually entered as passive variables by sociologists concern primarily integration into sets of social relationships predating the investigation. According to these positions shared with others, individuals are supposed to actualize representations available in their social environment. Experimental social psychologists sometimes proceed differently. They may try to create experimental conditions that actualize organizing principles of SRs in their subjects. This was the approach one of us took to study inter-group representations and self-representations in boys and girls.

Illustration: Positional Effects and Experimental Homologies

An analysis of the literature led Lorenzi-Cioldi (1988a, 1991a) to distinguish between two ideal-typical notions of the social group: the *aggregate* group and the *collection* group. The members of an aggregate group would view themselves as relatively undifferentiated homogeneous individuals defining themselves more directly by the characteristics attributed to their group as a whole, while the members of a collection group would see themselves more as individuals, each with his or her own specificity, defining themselves by personal qualities that would characterize them independently of their social membership. In our society, the aggregate group would tend to be female and occupy a dominated position, while the collection group would be male and occupy a dominating position.

The links between collection and aggregate groups on the one hand

and sex groups on the other were illustrated by Lorenzi-Cioldi by means of various experiments, one of which is summarized here. This experiment was conducted collectively in several classes of a secondary school. The experimenter told the subjects (boys and girls) that the aim of this research was to measure the autonomy and originality of individuals. After completing a self-description task on a semantic differential, the subjects were divided (apparently according to their responses but actually at random) into two groups. The experimenter made the first group believe that an analysis of the responses showed that some pupils had responded very differently from each other, while he told the second group that they had responded very similarly. Each pupil therefore belonged to a group called 'Different ones' or a group called 'Similar ones'.

According to the above definition, collection and aggregate groups are thus defined by their respective status as well as by different degrees of interpersonal homogeneity. The experimental memberships reflect the opposition between the singularization of the self ('Different ones' group; collection group) and interpersonal uniformity or homogeneity ('Similar ones' group; aggregate group). The 'Different ones' thus have dominating characteristics such as originality, autonomy and distinctiveness of the self in the group. The 'Similar ones', by contrast, have non-dominating characteristics such as lack of differentiation and interchangeability in the group. This study thus involved an experimental induction of organizing principles in connection with status differences between dominating and dominated ones, men and women, individuals considering themselves different from others and typical, and individuals defined by collective similarity.

The results reported by Lorenzi-Cioldi (1988a, 93–121) showed the effectiveness of such an induction and bore out the hypothesis of homology between groups with heterogeneous contents and meanings: groups of boys and groups of 'Different ones', on the one hand, and groups of girls and groups of 'Similar ones', on the other, join together preferentially. The social-identity processes in the two groupings considered – the experimental grouping (collection–aggregate groups) and the more lasting and natural memberships (boys–girls groups) – should reflect each other and, in given circumstances, superimpose each other. The hypothesis of homology thus links together the effects of two distinct kinds of memberships, that is sex groups and experimental groups (collection and aggregate).

CFA is especially helpful to investigate such homologies because it can produce a joint space of targets and of social and experimental subjects' locations. Let us illustrate this homology using the results of an experiment in which subjects were asked to describe themselves, their ingroup, the outgroup, someone of their ingroup and someone of the outgroup. We give here the results for descriptions made on scales presented as common, i.e., the subjects were told that the members of both groups considered them to be relevant to the description of the self. The four scales were, in fact, chosen because they represented a positive (communicative) and negative (subordinate) relational pole and a positive (autonomous) and negative (meticulous) instrumental pole.

CFA was performed with ratings of all the targets for all the scales as active variables and sex and experimental memberships ('Different ones' versus 'Similar ones') as passive variables. Individuals were placed in rows, while targets, experimental conditions and subjects' sex, representing active modalities (targets) and passive modalities (sex and experimental conditions), were placed in columns (see Table 8.1). Let us recall that the passive elements do not intervene in factor definition and that they are projected onto the axes resulting from an analysis of active elements. We will discuss here only the column modalities.

Figure 8.2 displays active variables (targets) and Figure 8.3 displays passive variables (experimental conditions and subjects' sex).

The responses in the common dimension clearly express an evaluative rating of the ingroup targets and the outgroup targets in favour of the former near the right of the graph (e.g., autonomous ingroup and subordinate outgroup) and in favour of the latter near the left of the graph (e.g., subordinate ingroup and autonomous outgroup). The sex and experimental memberships are evenly distributed from one pole to the other of this space according to their homologies. The congruent memberships accentuate the effects – points placed near the extremities of the two axes – while the incongruent memberships weaken and end up cancelling the effects of each membership taken separately – points placed near the origin of the axes.

These analyses generally reveal the harmony of the two types of memberships: sex and experimental (collection or aggregate groups). When subjects' memberships are homologous, the observed effects are far more pronounced: in these situations and for both sexes, there is no contradiction or incompatibility between the connotations associated with the two groups. When the memberships are incongruent, however, the subjects of both sexes tend to give the judgements that are typical of the members of their experimental group (judgements consequently typical of the sex outgroup). These results thus tend to conceptualize the sex differences as differences associated with social status, i.e., with types of intra- and inter-group relationships. They show especially that experimentally created situations can actualize organizing principles that govern the symbolic relationships between sex groups but are also sensitive to variations entered into these relationships. It is in this sense that one can speak of homologous relationships between experimental conditions and subjects' usual social integration. These results also

Table 8.1 CFA of ratings of targets: coordinates and absolute and relative contributions of active modalities (targets) and passive modalities (experimental conditions and subjects' sex)

	Factor							
	1				2			
	Order	Co-ordinate	RCO (%)	CTR (%)	Order	Co-ordinate	RCO (%)	CTR (%)
DIFFERENT ONES/BOYS	1	0.43	4.90	2.9	38	−0.56	8.43	10.1
DIFFERENT ONES	4	0.26	6.78	2.5	35	−0.24	5.85	4.4
BOYS	5	0.22	3.19	1.4	34	−0.24	3.73	3.4
og/subordinate	6	0.20	59.03	11.9	20	0.01	0.00	0.0
po/subordinate	7	0.19	46.28	10.5	14	0.07	6.37	2.9
s/autonomous	8	0.18	49.21	10.8	22	−0.03	1.33	0.6
DIFFERENT ONES/GIRLS	11	0.13	0.76	0.4	21	−0.01	0.00	0.0
ig/autonomous	12	0.12	26.77	4.8	25	−0.07	8.62	3.1
pi/autonomous	13	0.09	20.83	2.6	24	−0.05	5.96	1.5
po/meticulous	14	0.08	8.35	1.7	29	−0.08	10.47	4.2
ig/communicative	15	0.05	8.59	0.9	15	0.06	11.65	2.3
s/communicative	16	0.04	3.35	0.5	13	0.08	14.66	4.6
pi/communicative	17	0.04	4.29	0.5	18	0.04	3.62	0.9
og/meticulous	18	0.03	1.65	0.2	27	−0.08	10.47	3.1
ig/meticulous	19	0.01	0.17	0.0	17	0.05	5.67	1.4
pi/meticulous	22	−0.01	0.06	0.0	19	0.02	0.51	0.2
SIMILAR ONES/BOYS	23	−0.02	0.01	0.0	9	0.13	0.38	0.5
s/meticulous	24	−0.02	0.72	0.2	12	0.09	9.37	4.0
po/communicative	25	−0.08	11.51	2.2	32	−0.15	36.74	14.4
og/communicative	26	−0.09	14.53	2.9	33	−0.16	42.20	17.0
pi/subordinate	27	−0.09	11.09	2.4	6	0.17	36.41	16.0
GIRLS	29	−0.14	2.73	0.9	7	0.17	3.91	2.5
ig/subordinate	32	−0.15	31.35	5.9	8	0.14	28.08	10.7
s/subordinate	33	−0.21	40.75	11.2	11	0.12	12.78	7.1
og/autonomous	34	−0.22	57.40	14.9	26	−0.07	5.66	3.0
po/autonomous	35	−0.23	61.03	15.9	28	−0.07	5.98	3.1
SIMILAR ONES	36	−0.26	6.12	2.4	3	0.26	6.11	4.9
SIMILAR ONES/GIRLS	38	−0.41	6.88	3.8	1	0.34	4.71	5.2
% of variance		26.80				13.20		

Note: Targets:
s = self
pi = person of ingroup
po = person of outgroup
ig = ingroup
og = outgroup

Abbreviations: RCO = relative contributions
CTR = absolute contributions

The passive elements are in capital letters. The sum of absolute contributions is 100 per cent, excluding the passive elements.

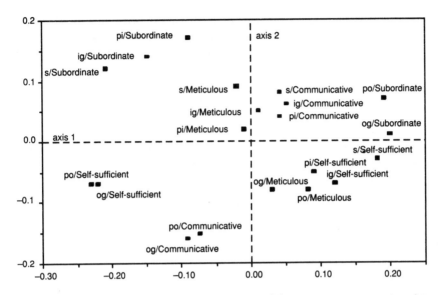

Figure 8.2   *Graphic representation of active modalities (targets) on axes 1 and 2 of CFA (ratings of self, ingroup and outgroup).*

Abbreviations: s   =   *self*
                      pi =   *person of ingroup*
                      po =   *person of outgroup*
                      ig =   *ingroup*
                      og =   *outgroup*

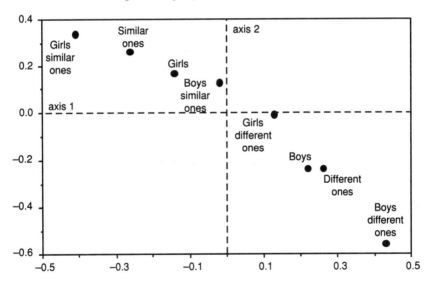

Figure 8.3   *Graphic representation of passive modalities (subjects' membership groups) on axes 1 and 2 of CFA.*

suggest that the representations of individuals (boys and girls) do not have this rigid characteristic attributed to them by a research tradition that makes sex opposition a natural inclination coded into the individual.

Illustration: Letters of Denunciation

Let us see another adaptation of CFA with passive variables. Boltanski (1984) performed it while studying letters to the Editor of the French newspaper *Le Monde*. We cannot describe here all of the 106 active variables chosen. These were partly based on the following analysis of the 'agent' system of denunciatory letters: 'Denunciation initiates, in fact, a relationship system between four agents: (1) denouncer, (2) beneficiary of denunciation, (3) denouncee and (4) agents to whom denunciation is made.' Each of the four agents occupies a specific position on a continuum that ranges from the most individual to the most collective. Thus, for example, the agents to which denunciation is made may be located on this continuum:

> ... it may be a single individual (e.g., denouncing to a woman the behaviour of her husband trying to dispossess her of an inheritance for the benefit of his mistress) or, at the opposite pole, a collective entity empowered to represent the whole of mankind (e.g., denouncing at the UN rostrum, i.e., 'to the whole world', the 'genocide of the Armenian people by the Turks'). Many agents occupy an intermediate position between these two extremes: denunciation to the parapolice or the secret police is more singular, for instance, than denunciation (deposition) to the examining magistrate that may have to be repeated in public, and denunciation to the political committee of a party is more singular than denunciation to the general assembly or the congress, etc. (Boltanski, 1984, 6–7).

While a first axis of CFA opposes the letters according to the degree of proximity between agents, i.e., according to the degree to which the relationship linking them together is singular, a second axis expresses the agents' position on the continuum ranging from the singular to the collective. It opposes cases involving single individuals as principal agents who did not use collective resources to cases involving collective entities as principal agents, or their representatives, and in which many collective resources (such as associations, courts and newspapers) were used.

Of particular interest is the projection of passive variables on to the space formed by these two axes. These variables were first formed by judgements given by six judges on 275 letters. These judges were instructed to read the letters quickly and rate the degree of normality of their authors from 1 (completely normal) to 10 (completely mad). It turned out, in fact, that the verdict of 'normality' was spontaneously given by the journalists in charge of processing the letters to the Editor.

Technically, this passive variable amounted to counting the number of times a specific rating was given by the six judges to each letter. It is therefore clear that many ratings had zero frequency. Here are the results of this analysis:

> The normality ratings are distributed in an orderly manner on the diagonal of the factor space. They rise evenly as one moves from affairs handled collectively and whose participants have no personal relationship on to affairs involving individuals already linked by vested relationships (and especially by family ties) and having to be managed entirely by the victim him-/herself without the aid of collective resources . . . (ibid., 14)

In other words, the representation of the normality of the authors of these letters depends on the public nature of the cause. It is normal for an association of residents to denounce in a letter to the Editor of *Le Monde* expulsions of residents by a real-estate company. It is abnormal to write a letter recounting gossip that circulates in a given social milieu. Another source of representation of abnormality is the status gap between different agents:

> The wider the position gap in different agents between the singular and the collective, the more denunciation is likely to be perceived as abnormal: it is abnormal, for instance, for a father to write a political programme designed solely for his children; it is abnormal to send a letter to the police denouncing the machinations of the dominant social class in general. It is also abnormal for a single individual to denounce publicly, by means of a letter to the press, his/her son's disrespect for him/her. (ibid., 14–15)

The projection of occupational origins as a passive variable also proved instructive. For example, whereas professors, writers and artists testified for others, executives, small-business owners, craftsmen, storekeepers, farmers and especially employees or staff members wrote in their name alone and made denunciations to their advantage.

Let us conclude this section on CFA used to differentiate between groups of individuals against the background of shared representations. In fact, this technique presupposes the existence of a representational field while showing that groups of individuals occupy different places therein. We have also seen that these variations can be produced experimentally. Even in this case, CFA is still suited for analyzing the anchoring of representations in symbolic relations whose complexity is systematically controlled. Thus, the conception of SRs as rigid and con-sensual images is certainly outdated, but the idea of differences or varia-tions in positioning in relation to common notional reference points is still valid. Other analytic techniques, such as automatic interaction detection, discriminant analysis and determination of subgroups' cen-tres of gravity, will not belie this general conception.

9

Factor Scores:
Anchoring of Individual Variations

Multiple correspondence analysis (MCA) with its passive elements is essentially similar to principal-component analysis (PCA) for which one calculates individual positions or factor scores on each factor.

In factor analysis, calculating the means of factor scores for all individuals enables us to project the 'centres of gravity' (means of subgroups of respondents) into the spaces defined by the dimensions revealed by the analysis. Moreover, appropriate analyses of variance allow us to conclude that there may be significant differences between the subgroups of a study population.

Illustration: Mirror Identities

An example of this approach was provided by Lorenzi-Cioldi and Meyer (1984) while analyzing the results of a study conducted in Geneva, Switzerland. The study involved 300 Swiss and 218 Italian and Spanish pupils (second-generation children of Italian and Spanish immigrants), aged 15–16, in the final year of compulsory education in Geneva. In the first phase of the study, the subjects were asked to rate the applicability of twenty traits to the following five targets: *yourself, the Swiss in general, the foreigners in general, your friends* and *your compatriots*. The traits constituted a subset of a scale developed by Peabody (1968) and used many times in studies of national or ethnic stereotypes (see, for example, Peabody, 1985). The targets were presented simultaneously, and the ratings were given in dichotomic terms (applicable/inapplicable) for each target.

In a factor analysis of subjects' responses to the targets' characteristics proposed to them, it was from the third factor on that differential attributions appeared according to the relationship between respondents' social memberships and the nature of the rated groups. Because of the large number of variables included in the analysis and the complexity of their interrelations, we favoured analyzing the projection of certain targets on to factors 3 and 4 (see Doise and Lorenzi-Cioldi, 1991, Figure 1).

A major difference appeared in the ratings given by subjects to different targets. For the targets *yourself, your friends* and *your compatriots*, the descriptive component predominated. Pairs of characteristics describing similar behaviour and with opposite evaluative connotations tended to covary in the same subspace. Example:

> *Thrifty* (+) and *Stingy* (–) were opposed to *Generous* (+) and *Wasteful* (–).

All these characteristics were, however, similarly saturated unlike those reflecting the ratings of the targets *the Swiss in general* and *the foreigners in general*. The differences in factor scores revealed by an analysis of variance were thus apparently associated with differences in more objective rating. On the other hand, the ratings of the targets *the Swiss in general* and *the foreigners in general* appeared highly saturated with the evaluative component. Pairs of characteristics describing antithetic behaviour and with identical evaluative connotations covaried in the same subspace. Example:

> *Thrifty* (+) and *Generous* (+) were opposed to *Stingy* (–) and *Wasteful* (–).

We can now associate this structure with the respondents according to their social memberships. If we consider the nationality of subjects whose analysis of variance indicated the force of contrast on the two factors, the responses of the Swiss and foreign subjects were perfectly symmetrical. In fact, the Italian and Spanish pupils rated *the Swiss in general* negatively and *the foreigners in general* positively, while the Swiss pupils and, to a lesser extent, the pupils of 'other' nationalities rated *the foreigners in general* negatively and *the Swiss in general* positively.

Considering the fact that, in our sample population, the foreign subjects placed in the 'Others' category represented the privileged fringe of the foreigners living in Switzerland and that, very often, in the other areas of our questionnaire, they were in their behaviour fairly close to the Swiss subjects, we can interpret this factor as the emergence of response behaviour based on the expression of an ethnocentric sentiment. Such an ethnocentric dimension involving the appearance of ingroup favouritism (or so-called group self-idealization) is the index of salience, in the subjects, of the evocation of nationality-based groups. Ethnocentric functioning is, moreover, symmetrical, except for the 'other' subjects who are close to the origin of the axes in our results and thus do not occupy any significant position from this angle.

Let us stress the significance of the above approach. One and the same evaluative principle clearly organized individual positioning in rating *the foreigners in general* and *the Swiss in general.* Depending on the target, however, the members of different national groups applied this organization inversely. Of course, it was, in a way, a banal result demonstrating the intervention of a strong ethnocentric sentiment, although this sentiment often seemed to show itself only with regard to general categories (see, in this respect, Doise and Lorenzi-Cioldi, 1991). The important thing is to indicate how the centres-of-gravity technique makes it possible to show the variation in the positions occupied by members of different national groups while using nearly identical factor dimensions. This is therefore another illustration of the fact that differences between SRs can often be viewed as the application of the same organizing principles, but from different positions. In the present case, these positions simply invert ratings according to targets.

Illustration: Parental Experiences and Naïve Conceptions of Intelligence

Here is another example of the frequent use of centres-of-gravity calculations for establishing links between SRs and social positions. Mugny and Carugati (1989) studied the effects of parental experience on SRs of intelligence. The authors pondered the following question:

> In what ways is parental experience likely to be able to influence representations of intelligence? Our answer to this is directly related to the conception of social representations as familiarisations of the unfamiliar [. . .]. The idea is really very simple, although it also has a great many serious consequences: the child constitutes, in a sense, an element of unfamiliarity within the family nucleus. He is unfamiliar because he is unpredictable. Quite apart from the unpredictability of appearance, there is no way of anticipating personality, character, ways of behaving, or even intelligence, with any degree of certainty. In this chapter we shall try to show the effects of what we regard as a parental identity, which has its own ways of operating, event though, of course it is liable to be modified by sociological variables (Mugny and Carugati, 1989, 95)

Later (ibid., 102), this hypothesis was specified for parental experience intensified by the birth of a second child: 'We know that all children are different (apart from monozygotic twins), whether they are brothers or sisters. This renewal of inter-individual differences ought therefore to accentuate further the representation of intelligence typical of parental experience.' One also considers that the fact of having children adds to the experience (already restructuring these representations) of 'transition from being a student to being a responsible teacher' (ibid., 138).

Let us now relate the results obtained by comparing the means of the factor scores achieved by different subgroups of the study population to a first factor obtained by factor-analyzing sixty-six questions about intelligence in general. This factor, which accounted for 10.2 per cent of variance before rotation, was described by the authors as follows (ibid., 50):

> It is based essentially on the theory of natural inequality and giftedness; genetic inheritance seems to play an important part in it, but so also do the attitudes to intelligence developed within the family. The concept can thus be defined by the following synthesis: intelligence is a gift which is divided unequally among the population; intelligence needs to be protected by a policy of discrimination, particularly in schools (which is where, it seems to us, this concept establishes itself as ideology); intelligence is defined as a sum total of mental and social aptitudes which enable the child to succeed at school, especially in subjects with a high educational valency (like mathematics); these aptitudes develop through the attitudes to intelligence which obtain within the family; intelligence, finally, is largely a question of biology, or even morphobiology.

Mugny and Carugati were thus able to verify their hypotheses by comparing the means of the factor scores obtained by different subgroups on this factor centring on the theory of natural inequality and gift. As a matter of fact, for groups of non-parents and parents, these mean scores were −0.13 and +0.29 (p<0.001) respectively. For parents with only one child, the mean score was +0.11 versus +0.39 for parents with at least two children (p<0.02). An analysis involving only teachers showed that they were generally rather sceptical about the theory of natural gift, but less so when they had children (mean score: −0.02) than when they were childless (mean score: −0.31; p<0.007).

Illustration: Adults' Representations of Children

A last example of the use of factor scores was provided by Verquerre's research (1989) on the representations which adults, and especially parents, hold about children. We will present here only a small part of the results of a survey conducted using a questionnaire of thirty-one bipolar scales on a sample population of 320 parents divided into eight groups stratified by two variables: sex and sociocultural background. The parents were asked to give their opinion about children in general. We will first summarize the overall results of this survey and highlight the factors that structured the representations of children for the whole sample population. We will then report the variations in these representations according to the mothers' sociocultural background.

Three factors structured the adults' representations of children:

1 A factor centring on the possibilities of children's capacity of control and rational adjustment to reality.
2 A factor whose meaning was fairly similar to that of the Introversion–Extroversion factor and centring on the possibilities of creation and expression of children. This factor had a dual orientation and expressed parental concern about the positive and negative aspects of children's expansiveness.
3 A factor centring on children's affectivity.

Verquerre (1989) did not limit his analysis to this overview. He also ran principal-component analyses (PCAs) for various subgroups defined by their sex and membership in different sociocultural groups. His survey involved, in fact, four groups of mothers and four groups of fathers of different sociocultural backgrounds (backgrounds 1 most favoured, 2 intermediate, 3 most disadvantaged and 4 rural).

Table 9.1 summarizes the results obtained for the groups of mothers by indicating each time the three scales that contributed most to the selected factors.

For the four groups, one found the same factor structure already revealed by a PCA of the whole sample population. The factors also, however, presented real specificities according to the different groups. Thus, the first factor of the PCA of the mothers of background 1 proved specific in that it integrated into its definition such scales as *unfinished–finished* and *irresponsible–responsible*. The mothers of background 1 seemed primarily concerned about the autonomy of which children are capable. The mothers of background 2, by contrast, primarily assessed the possibilities of control in children, whereas the mothers of background 3 also rated the affective qualities of children. For them, the scales *bad–good* and *cruel–kind*, for example, greatly helped define the first factor. For the mothers of rural background, the first factor had overall a highly evaluative nature and also expressed their concern about the moral qualities of children, as shown by the presence of the scales *imperfect–perfect* and *hypocritical–frank*.

Let us now see how these differences were analyzed in more detail. An analysis of variance was performed on the ratings of the three factors of the PCA obtained from the whole sample population. The background variable yielded very significant results for factors 1 and 3. This is another illustration of centres-of-gravity calculations. To make the nature of these differences clearer, however, different subgroups were compared for the gross ratings given by subjects to the different scales.

Table 9.1 PCA results for representations of children by four groups of mothers: percentage of explained variance of the first three factors and scales with the highest loadings on these factors

	Factor		
	1	2	3
Background 1	23.99% Unfinished–Finished Unreasonable–Reasonable Irresponsible–Responsible	13.24% Soft–Hard Passive–Active Withdrawn–Outgoing	11.51% Insensitive–Sensitive Unimaginative–Imaginative Sad–Cheerful
Background 2	20.01% Disorderly–Orderly Boisterous–Quiet Dirty–Clean	11.51% Weak–Strong Hypocritical–Frank Passive–Active	8.77% Bad–Good Sad–Cheerful Cruel–Kind
Background 3	21.36% Unstable–Stable Disobedient–Obedient Unfinished–Finished	10.67% Quiet–Boisterous Irresponsible–Responsible Withdrawn–Outgoing	9.14% Unaffectionate–Affectionate Strong–Weak Unpleasant–Pleasant
Background rural 4	24.60% Imperfect–Perfect Disorderly–Orderly Hypocritical–Frank	15.09% Unimaginative–Imaginative Shy–Sure of oneself Quiet–Boisterous	10.03% Insensitive–Sensitive Unaffectionate–Affectionate Poor–Rich

(According to Verquerre, 1989)

Table 9.2 *Representations of children by groups of mothers: scales yielding a significant difference in means between rural background and various urban backgrounds*

Comparisons		
Background 1	Background 2	Background 3
Lazy–Courageous	Lazy–Courageous	Lazy–Courageous
Imperfect–Perfect	Imperfect–Perfect	Poor–Rich
Dirty–Clean	Dirty–Clean	Unfinished–Finished
Disorderly–Orderly	Disorderly–Orderly	Unstable–Stable
Unfinished–Finished	Unfinished–Finished	
Homely–Handsome	Unreasonable–Reasonable	
	Unstable–Stable	
	Homely–Handsome	

Note: All significant differences yielded higher scores (right-hand pole of the scale) for
mothers of rural background.
(According to Verquerre, 1989)

Of course, this latter comparison would have been just as feasible without using factor analysis. This latter method, however, enables an overall meaning to be given to a multitude of differences. As explained in Chapter 2, the position of a scale on a factor should not be confused with the degree of agreement or disagreement shown by respondents. Thus, the two ways of looking at responses complement each other. To illustrate the results of this approach, Table 9.2 shows the scales that revealed in the same mothers significant differences between rural backgrounds and various urban backgrounds.

Scales yielding significant differences generally concerned the possibilities of control and rational adjustment to reality of children, and the mothers of rural background thus obtained the highest scores. Let us also note that the two indicators used (factor ratings and gross ratings) revealed highly homogeneous results for the mothers of various sociocultural backgrounds within the urban background. The sociocultural variable hardly modified the orientation of the representations of children. On the contrary, compared with the mothers of urban background but with differences according to the sociocultural comparison group, the mothers of rural background considered children to be more orderly. We have already observed that the mothers of rural background presented a fairly specific factor structure and appeared particularly attentive to the moral qualities of children. In rural background, the representations of children appeared to centre more on control and conformism, and the geographic variable proved more differentiating for the representations of children and notably its value orientation than the social–cultural variable as such.

10

Automatic Interaction Detection:

Hierarchization of Field Divisions

Social memberships, social positions and adherence to certain beliefs may be interwoven in a complex manner. There are various techniques for sorting out these factors and determining their relative importance in the actualization of certain organizing principles of SRs. We will now discuss automatic interaction detection.

Automatic interaction detection requires a fairly large sample population. It seeks systematically to determine which independent variables divide, before all others, a given sample population into two subgroups so that, for a dependent variable (factor scores for example), the difference between these two subgroups may be the greatest possible while achieving maximum homogeneity within the two subgroups. The procedure is repeated for each of the subgroups with the remaining independent variables or the remaining partitions of the already entered independent variables. Each subgroup may, if necessary, be further subdivided into two different segments. They may then be no longer the same independent variables that divide each subgroup already formed. The procedure is discontinued when a series of subdivisions result in the formation of subgroups that are too small or when the differences between subgroups become negligible.

Illustration: Topics of Family Conversation

To illustrate the general principle of the above procedure, we will now present the results of an analysis performed on topics of conversation of Swiss secondary schoolers with their parents (Doise, 1985). For sixteen topics, the pupils indicated if they discussed them more or less often at home.

A PCA provided the dependent variable. As it had yielded an uninteresting first factor by obtaining positive and significant loadings for all items, we chose the factor scores on the second factor for analysis. This factor, which accounted for 11.3 per cent of total variance, yielded positive loadings of at least 0.20 for five topics: Communism (0.63), politics (0.63), art (0.45), living 'out in the country' (0.34) and community life (0.25), and negative loadings for four topics: outing (–0.51), clothing (–0.39), leisure activities (–0.32) and money (–0.24). The factor thus opposed topics further removed from daily concerns (positive pole) to more specific topics (negative pole).

Automatic interaction detection was performed with five independent variables: the pupils' nationality (Swiss, Spanish, Italian or others), sex, the socioeconomic level of their family (upper, middle and lower), their scholastic section (General, Latin–Modern and Science) and the four secondary schools attended.

The aim of this study was therefore to see which of these five variables divided the sample population into two subgroups during a first division. As shown by Figure 10.1, the first differentiation obtained separated the pupils of the General section (mean score: –0.21) from those of the other sections (mean score: +0.22) – a significant difference at a threshold of 0.001. The results thus obtained were the same as those observed many times previously and confirmed the taste of the pupils of

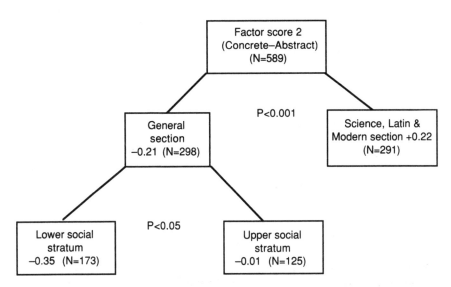

Figure 10.1 *Graphic representation of results of automatic interaction detection on family conversations.*

Note: This analysis was performed on the second factor score of family conversations. This figure indicates the subdivision level (independent variable), the statistical significance of subdivision, the deviation from the mean factor score (0) and the number of subjects of each subdivision.

'prestigious' scholastic sections for the abstract (see Deschamps, Lorenzi-Cioldi and Meyer, 1982). An analysis of the pupils of the Science and Latin–Modern sections revealed no significant difference at a threshold of 0.05 either according to their social origin (significant trend at 0.10) or according to their sex, nationality or secondary schools attended. An analysis of the pupils of the General section, by contrast, showed another division according to their social origin: the pupils of 'lower' social origin (mean score: –0.35) differed significantly (at a threshold of 0.05) from all the other pupils (mean score: –0.01). The pupils of 'middle' or 'upper' social origin who found themselves in a section sociologically less suitable for them were thus closer to the pupils of the more prestigious sections in their responses to a test that evoked the family universe.

These results illustrated well the general principle of automatic interaction detection: this method detects the independent variables best suited for forming subgroups that are internally homogeneous and different between themselves. This variable is the scholastic section here. Then it also yields effects of interaction between variables: combined with prestigious sections, no other independent variable produces any subsequent differentiations, while the socioeconomic variable produces a differentiating effect between pupils of the less prestigious section.

Illustration: On-campus Progressivism and Conservatism

Automatic interaction detection was also performed by Francès (1980) to study on-campus ideology. Let us first specify some characteristics of this study: it did not involve the typical French university in its entirety but two Parisian universities offering degrees in social sciences only. The questionnaire used for this research concerned attitudes towards institutions and their standards and values: marriage and parental authority in the family, the Church, the law, the Army and socioeconomic institutions (such as large private enterprises, taxation and free trade). A first survey involved 720 first- and third-year undergraduates at Paris Nanterre, while a second survey involving 364 undergraduates at different sections of Paris Centre verified the main results of the first survey.

The author did not base this research on any SR studies. The first factor obtained by CFA for the two sample populations, however, can be related to an organizing principle intervening often in SRs because it located the respondents on an axis ranging from the acceptance and defence of institutions (negative pole) to the criticism and rejection of institutions and their values (positive pole).

The author described this axis as follows:

> Along the negative part of the axis, one found, starting from its
> extremity, the vigorous defence of the Church, the law, the Army,
> the family, large private enterprises, direct taxation such as the
> one that existed at the time of the survey and authoritarian edu-
> cation of children. These subjects were practising believers, had
> the same ideas as their parents and were happy living with their
> parents. It may be admitted that, in this negative part, there was a
> certain hierarchization of attitudes because concerning one and
> the same item, extreme assertions were found near the extremity
> and more moderate assertions near the centre . . . Along the
> positive part of the axis, one found, starting from the periphery
> towards the centre, a series of rejections of political institutions
> (national elections), marriage, the Church, the Army, the law,
> parental authority in the education of children and free trade. It
> was found that, in these rejections, the Church and the Army
> were more polar than the other institutions, which was
> symmetrical to the negative part of this axis. On the other hand,
> it was found that the attitudes towards parental authority and
> disciplining of children to obedience, while being opposed, were
> not so discriminating as the attitudes towards the Church and the
> Army. In any event, the subjects close to this part of the axis
> declared not being religious and never agreeing with their
> parents. (Francès, 1980, 78–81)

The various university departments where the subjects were studying
were entered into CFA as passive variables by taking account of
progress in their studies (first or third year). Starting from the negative
pole, one encountered successively two groups of the Departments of
German and Law, two groups of the Departments of Economic Sciences,
English and Spanish, and then very close to the origin, the sole
Geography group that was questioned at Nanterre. Starting from the
origin and moving along the positive part of the axis, one found the
History, Arts, Psychology, Philosophy and Sociology groups.

This order has a meaning: it coincides with the percentage of votes in
favour of student movements that are located by expert judges more to
the right or to the left on a political continuum. However, automatic
interaction detection was performed to understand better the meaning
of this distribution of the various university departments on the first
axis of CFA.

The theoretical question asked was the following: do the undergraduates at the various departments differ from each other because they have
received different types of education or have they chosen these different
types of education because they had different attitudes towards the

institutions? In the latter case, one may ponder the origin of these attitudes: are they directly induced by socioeconomic class memberships or are they modulated by other factors?

The first term of the alternative can easily be ruled out: in fact, progress in the studies does not produce systematic differences in the projection of groups on to the axis of CFA. Progress in the studies therefore does not seem to affect subjects' position on the axis considered. Automatic interaction detection, however, provides interesting information on the intervention of other factors. This detection was performed on the scores on the first factor with the membership of the students in their respective departments as independent variables and fourteen other variables, including having a paid job, studies done after obtaining the secondary-school diploma, reasons for choosing the current studies, the family circle's influence on this choice, satisfaction with the education received, parents' occupation, sex, major characteristics of the profession considered and number of years of studies.

The results of this detection for the undergraduates at Paris Nanterre showed first the importance of being part of the university departments: a first interaction detection differentiated between the Departments of German, Law, Spanish, Economic Sciences, English and Geography with a negative mean score on the one hand, and the Departments of History, Arts, Psychology, Philosophy and Sociology with a positive mean score on the other. Further interaction detections of all those questioned, however, also showed significant differences of which the three most important in decreasing order were: between those who asserted that, above all, material advantages are important in the profession considered (negative mean score) and all the others, those who chose their studies according to the predictable career prospects (negative mean score) and all the others, and those who answered that their father practised a liberal profession or was a top executive or those who did not answer this question (negative mean score) versus all the others.

These results suggest the prime importance of two motivations governing the choice of studies (expected advantages and career prospects) and, apparently to a lesser extent, of the father's occupation.

Other pieces of information were provided by the division between students who belonged to the group of the six 'conservative' departments and between those who belonged to the other five departments. For the former, the most important dichotomy turned out to be between those who expressed a certain satisfaction with the education received or who did not answer the question (negative mean score) and those who were dissatisfied with their education (positive mean score). However, further significant, albeit less important, divisions were made according to the career prospects going hand in hand with interest in the studies, expected material advantages and the father's occupation.

> In conclusion, at the more or less conservative departments, the ideology continuum was well correlated with social origin, but this determinant was amply modulated by intrinsic motives that were dictated by occupational plans, the degree of their realizability and link with the studies chosen to realize them and the materialistic or intellectual value system underlying this choice. Between these elements of occupational plans and 'existential' conservatism, there was also an affinity with ideological conservatism. In fact, interest in the subject matter taught and intellectual activities associated with the future profession go hand in hand with a certain conservatism. They are not the same as in the whole sample population. (Francès, 1980, 148–9)

Moreover, while the climate of opinion at the Departments of Arts and Social Sciences was thus protest-oriented, this tendency was more pronounced in boys who were dissatisfied with their studies. It was tempered in girls, especially of favoured social origin, who had no need of a paid job.

The work of Francès (1980) included results on other components of on-campus ideology. We have reported here those that enable us best to illustrate the relevance of automatic interaction detection for studying the anchoring of organizing principles of SRs.

11

Discriminant Analysis:
Field Organization by Groups

SRs are not necessarily studied as unique representational fields in which groups are located in different places. Some researchers set out to detect a possible variation in the nature of representational fields in different groups. The significance of discriminant analysis lies in the fact that this procedure aims to test the degree of homogeneity within groups of individuals while seeking to make a maximum distinction between these groups. This analysis predicts the membership of individuals in their respective groups by using their responses to a number of questions. This type of analysis thus seeks to produce functions that are interpreted as factor dimensions apart from the fact that they offer response configurations enabling us to distinguish between groups of individuals as well as possible, while the factors of factor analysis allow us to distinguish between individuals (see Part Two). Thus, discriminant functions, as indicated by their name, are factors of sorts subjected to the additional constraint of differentiating between groups of individuals while maximizing the homogeneity of individuals within the groups.

Thus, whereas factor analysis summarizes inter-individual variations, discriminant analysis summarizes inter-group variations. Individual responses are integrated into functions according to their ability to discriminate between groups of subjects.

Discriminant analysis is a flexible technique. It is generally used in two ways. To test the homogeneity of groups of subjects, one compares the distribution of the subjects within these groups determined by the analysis (predicted groups) with their actually observed distribution. The more both distributions are superposed, the more one will be able to conclude that the borderlines between the groups are clear-cut and that these groups are associated with specific fields. We will give two illustrations of this application. Discriminant analysis can also be used to describe inter-group differences. In this case, one will look into discriminant scores and the contributions of variables to functions in order to accentuate the characteristics that distinguish between groups.

Discriminant Analysis and Homogeneity of Social Groups

Illustration: Determinants of the Choice of an Occupation

We will first take an example again from the data obtained from apprentices (see Part One). The subjects indicated the importance of ten items in the choice of an occupation on a four-point scale (very important, fairly important, hardly important and unimportant). The items were the following:

1 Ensuring oneself a stable future.
2 Having social contacts.
3 Earning a lot of money.
4 Doing something useful for others.
5 Having an occupation one likes.
6 Having a certain power.
7 Having responsibilities.
8 Acquiring a high social status and certain prestige.
9 Being able to use one's abilities.
10 Having leisure.

Let us ask ourselves if this set of items enables us to differentiate between subjects according to their training level. To find out, we will perform a discriminant analysis of their training level (three groups corresponding each to one of the three training levels) by entering their responses to the ten items as independent variables.

Since this analysis involves three groups of subjects, a maximum of two discriminant functions can be obtained.

Table 11.1 shows the main characteristics of these functions. The first function is considerably more powerful than the second. It accounts for more than three-quarters of the explained variance and reaches an acceptable statistical threshold.

Since the second function hardly differentiates between groups, we will perform a second discriminant analysis by selecting just one function. To interpret the results of this analysis, we will refer to the coefficients of different variables on the discriminant functions: the standardized coefficients enable us to find out how the function is oriented, while the non-standardized coefficients serve to calculate the scores of each subject and, consequently, to classify them in one of the groups. The weight of the variables in each discriminant function can be assessed by

Table 11.1   *Results of discriminant analysis of training level with determinants of the choice of an occupation: description of two discriminant functions*

Funct.	Eigenvalue	% Explained Variance	Wilks' Lambda	Chi-Square	d.l.	Sign.
1	0.1051	76.47	0.8766	31.68	20	0.047
2	0.0323	23.53	0.9687	7.65	9	0.569

Note: The eigenvalue corresponds to the relationship between inter- and intra-group variations. Wilks' Lambda indicates the percentage of variance not explained by inter-group differences. It is relatively high. This value enables a Chi-square to be calculated so as to test a hypothesis of equality between the mean discriminant scores

their correlation with the discriminant functions. Table 11.2 shows these correlations and the standardized coefficients of each of the variables on the first function.

One observes that the variables most closely correlated with the first function concern primarily what could be called the instrumental aspects of occupational activity (acquisition of privileges, in a way). These variables are the most discriminating, as evidenced by an analysis of variance performed for each of them with the training level as a source of variation. The variables correlated negatively with this first function – less differentiating than the others – relate more to the expressive aspects of occupational activity (doing what one likes, having leisure and social contacts). Reading the standardized coefficients of the variables on the first discriminant function shows that these two aspects are poles apart.

An observation of the mean scores obtained by the three groups on the first function – centroids – indicates that the instrumental aspects

Table 11.2   *Results of discriminant analysis of training level with determinants of the choice of an occupation: correlations of independent variables with the first discriminant function and standardized coefficients of these variables*

Variables	Correlations	Standardized coefficients
Acquiring a high social status	0.63	0.58
Earning a lot of money	0.55	0.53
Ensuring oneself a stable future	0.48	0.26
Having a certain power	0.35	−0.02
Having leisure	−0.26	−0.50
Having social contacts	−0.23	−0.15
Having an occupation one likes	−0.18	−0.24
Being useful to others	0.15	0.23
Having abilities	0.08	−0.20
Having responsibilities	0.12	−0.01

Table 11.3 *Results of discriminant analysis of training level with determinants of the choice of an occupation: centroids of three training levels*

Level	Centroid
1	–0.35
2	–0.04
3	0.46

become more important as the apprentices progress in their training.

To assess the predictive value of the discriminant functions, let us compare the distribution of individuals in the three groups obtained by discriminant analysis with the actually observed distribution.

Overall, 46 per cent of individuals are assigned to their current ingroup. How is this to be interpreted? A first possibility is to compare the number of correctly classified individuals with the number that would be obtained randomly. Thus, the likelihood of belonging to group 1 is 34 per cent, i.e., the percentage of subjects classified in the first year of apprenticeship. One finds that the percentage of individuals correctly predicted in group 1 by discriminant analysis is 48.2 per cent. A Chi-square calculated to compare the two percentages enables us to reject the hypothesis of equality at a threshold below $p = 0.05$ ($\chi^2(1) = 4.09$). One also finds that the number of subjects correctly classified in group 3 (44.4 per cent) is significantly larger than the number that would be obtained randomly (29 per cent) ($\chi^2(1) = 7.09$; $p<0.01$). On the other hand, the number of subjects correctly classified in group 2 (45.1 per cent) is not different from the number that would be obtained randomly (37 percent). As shown already by an observation of the centroids, discriminant analysis mainly differentiates between the two

Table 11.4 *Results of discriminant analysis of training level with determinants of the choice of an occupation: comparison of the number of apprentices observed and the number of apprentices predicted by discriminant analysis at different training levels*

	N	Group predicted Level 1	2	3
Group observed Level				
1	85	41	29	15
		48.2%	34.1%	17.6%
2	9l	30	41	20
		33.0%	45.1%	22.0%
3	72	16	24	32
		22.2%	33.3%	44.4%

extreme groups. This is not surprising. As it was found at the beginning of this chapter on statistical CFA, a first discriminant function (or a first dimension by analogy) always tends to oppose the extreme states of the analyzed data table to each other.

The second function therefore has the status of 'corrector'. In the present case, however, the behaviour of the mean group is not located homogeneously at the intersection of the behaviours of the subjects of the other groups. We will revert to this important point in the next example of the use of discriminant analysis. A second possibility of interpreting the results is to consider group 4, i.e., the subjects in the fourth year of training who were not included in discriminant analysis. One finds that they are mostly classified in group 3 (the difference from a random classification is insignificant: $\chi^2(1) = 2.89$; p<0.10).

Overall, one observes that the predicted classification confirms that the instrumental conception of occupational activity becomes more important when subjects progress in their training. To support this observation, let us add that the centroids of groups 3 and 4 are statistically different from those of groups 1 and 2 and that groups 1 and 2 also differ significantly.

Illustration: Topics of Conversation Among Friends

Another illustration of the effects of the use of discriminant analysis when groups of subjects can be roughly arranged on a continuum is provided by a question drawn from the above-mentioned survey of Deschamps, Lorenzi-Cioldi and Meyer (1982). Subjects indicated their interest in discussing nineteen topics or activities with their friends on a five-point scale ranging from 'never' to 'very often'. The items were the following:

1. Community life
2. Motorcycles
3. Hygiene
4. Money
5. Clothing
6. Alcohol
7. Choice of friends
8. Living out in the country
9. Communism
10. Art
11. Sexual experience
12. Politics
13. Professional life
14. Military service
15. Studies
16. Religion
17. Morals
18. Nights out
19. Leisure activities

The items were selected to present different aspects of the pupils' daily lives or, more specifically, to represent more or less concrete or abstract poles of thinking. Several authors have indeed shown that the degree of abstraction of discourses constitutes a major factor differentiating between social classes or backgrounds (see Bourdieu, 1977; Bernstein, 1975; Bisseret, 1974; and Espéret, 1979). The subjects were 200 boys and girls aged 14–15 and attached to three increasingly prestigious scholastic sections (a total of 350 subjects took part in the survey, but they did not all answer the same questions): Practical, Modern and Classics. It is impossible to describe the scholastic sections exhaustively in this book. Suffice it to say that the Practical section prepares its pupils for active life through apprenticeship and the practice of an occupation (like the subjects dealt with in the preceding example), while most pupils of the Classics section are destined to pursue long years of study (secondary-school diploma and university). The Modern section forms the intermediate category that interests us most in this example. Its evolution does not yet appear as clear-cut as that of the other two sections.

A discriminant analysis was performed for the nineteen items and the three groups of subjects. Since the analysis involved three groups of subjects as in the preceding example, we obtained a maximum of two discriminant functions. Two significant functions were chosen, accounting for 53 per cent of total variance, i.e. respectively 51 per cent of common variance for function 1 and 49 per cent of common variance for function 2. Contrary to what had happened in the preceding example, the two functions were therefore virtually equivalent. Their concurrent use was therefore fully justified. Function 1 opposed the items *Studies*, *Art* and *Politics* (positive pole) to the items *Professional life* and *Motorcycles* (negative pole). As shown by Table 11.5 that tabulates the centroids of the three groups on each function, this function opposed the Classics group, near the pole of the abstract, to the Modern and Practical groups, near the pole of the concrete.

Function 2 opposed *Living out in the country, Professional life, Choice of friends* and *Communism* (positive pole) to *Money, Hygiene, Community life* and *Sexual experience* (negative pole). The interesting aspect of this

Table 11.5 *Discriminant analysis results for scholastic section with the level of friendly conversations: centroids of scholastic groups*

	Centroid Function	
	1	2
Scholastic group		
Practical	−0.37	−0.87
Modern	−0.73	0.29
Classics	0.70	0.50

Table 11.6 *Discriminant analysis results for scholastic section with the level of friendly conversations: comparison of the number of pupils observed and the number of pupils predicted by the analysis in the different scholastic groups*

			Predicted group	
	N	Practical	Modern	Classics
Observed group				
Practical	67	44	9	14
		66%		
Modern	49	18	21	10
			43%	
Classics	84	12	8	64
				76%

Note: The percentages indicate the proportion of correctly predicted subjects.

analysis was the relative instability of the intermediate Modern group: close to the Practical group on function 1, it was close to the Classics group on the other function. Let us now consider the predictive value of the functions by means of Table 11.6.

The percentages of subjects correctly predicted in their current ingroups clearly show that the force of opposition between the two extreme categories, Classics and Practical, prevented or at least reduced the appearance and hence the adequate identification of the response profile of the Modern group. Most of the Modern group pupils were correctly placed in their group, but eighteen found themselves none the less in the lower category and ten in the upper category. When we performed three additional discriminant analyses, one for each pair of groups (these analyses thus involved two groups and provided a single discriminant function), we obtained the following results: for the Practical versus Modern opposition, the extracted function predicted the behaviour of 71 per cent of all individuals (the function accounted for 29 per cent of total variance); for the Classics versus Modern opposition, 79 per cent (33 per cent of explained variance); and finally for the Practical versus Classics opposition, 82 per cent (43 per cent of explained variance). In fact, while both the Classics and Practical groups showed interest in clearly opposite topics, the contents expressed by the Modern group became less specific as these contents were compared with those collected from the Practical group. The analyses performed thus enabled us to assign a position closer to the lower levels of the scholastic hierarchy to this intermediate group formed by the Modern section pupils.

Discriminant Analysis and Field Organization

Illustration: Representations of Mental Illness

An Italian study on SRs of mental illness (see Bellelli, 1987) used an investigative tool proposing closed opinion surveys on the definitions of mental illness, its causes and treatment. The results of this research were used by Zani (in press) to perform discriminant analyses on groups of subjects studying or working in the area of mental illness in three different cities. Seven groups were included in the first analysis: four groups of students (medicine, sciences, psychology and nursing care) and three groups of professionals (psychiatrists, psychologists and psychiatric nurses). Our colleague then ran analyses on the groups of students on the one hand and the groups of professionals on the other.

The first analysis enabled her to make a clear distinction between students and professionals using a single function accounting for over 50 per cent of variance (eigenvalue: 1.44, $p(\chi^2)$: 0.00001). It became especially apparent that the students considered that mental illness is characterized by progressive development and that it may be of biological origin, whereas the professionals laid more emphasis on the variety of its symptoms, such as periodicity of attacks and on the occurrence of acute phases.

For the students, the aims of therapy were to help mental patients establish social contacts and be accepted by society at large. The professionals were more concerned with alleviating the symptoms of the illness and enhancing patients' ability to satisfy the requirements of their social milieu through administration of therapeutic drugs and hospitalization. As for the most suitable places for treatment, however, the students considered that mental hospitals may also be effective, while the professionals stressed that mental patients must be treated within 'territorial structures' of mental health and at home in an environment familiar to them.

Discriminant analyses of subgroups of students and professionals made it possible to differentiate clearly between categories of subjects (71 per cent of subjects correctly classified in the first case and 90 per cent in the second).

Since they had received different types of education, the groups of students had different types of information on mental illness and its treatment. The first function (46 per cent of explained variance) opposed psychology students to all other groups, particularly to medical students and, to a lesser extent, to student nurses. The psychology students adhered to a psychosocial view of mental illness. They thought that its most effective treatment consists of changing the social environment and of family therapy, that the best suited places for therapy are apartment complexes and sectored care units, that the aim of treatment should be to develop patients' ability to establish social relationships and that the most serious consequence of mental illness is social isolation.

By contrast, the other three groups of subjects had a medicoclinical conception of mental illness: its causes would be of an individual nature and linked to biological factors; the use of therapeutic drugs would be the best treatment; and a general hospital should be considered the most suitable place for treating mental illness.

The second function (31 per cent of variance) differentiated between subgroups of student nurses and medical students. The former had a macrosocial view of mental illness and the latter a more medical conception. The third function (23 per cent of variance) opposed science students to the other groups, especially to medical and psychology students, the former having the peculiarity of adhering to a medicobiological view of mental illness that none the less laid less emphasis on its clinical aspects than did medical students.

Among the subgroups of professionals, the first function of discriminant analysis (63 per cent of variance) revealed, on the one hand, a medicosocial conception of mental illness with references to biological factors (alcoholism and drugs were considered to be causes, and the use of therapeutic drugs was recommended) and to social environmental factors (treatment required a change in the social environment and was designed to prevent patients from disturbing others); on the other hand there emerged a more institutionalized view of mental illness centring on the professional roles of physicians and diagnosticians. Nurses were at the first pole and psychologists at the second.

The second function (37 per cent of variance) opposed medico-organizational aspects (centring on hospital treatment with therapeutic drugs) to socio-relational aspects (family therapy). Psychiatrists were opposed to psychologists with nurses finding themselves between the other two groups.

Educational background, professional practices and goals thus clearly influence the way individuals are located in relation to the principal components of the representations of mental illness. Discriminant analysis thus enables us to verify to what extent the membership of individuals in certain groups can be predicted from differences between these groups in their representations themselves.

12

Correspondence Analysis of Textual Data

Various authors hypothesize that representations vary in the same individuals as a function of changes in their experiences. Experimentation is an ideal method for studying the dynamics of these changes, and it can use several of the techniques described in this book to form these dependent variables. We will end this chapter on anchoring, however, by illustrating a new technique that has proved useful for studying the relationship between representations and changes in occupational status during a comparative and non-experimental study designed primarily to test a new method of textual data analysis by CFA.

The research of Lorenzi-Cioldi (1991b) focused on comparing representations in two sexually mixed populations: students aiming at a given professional field and social workers.

Illustration: Anchoring of Social Work Representations

This study involved educators working for various institutions of the *Service Médico-Pédagogique* (SMP) of Geneva, Switzerland, and undergraduates at the Institute of Social Studies of Geneva intending to become specialized educators. Two open questions based on a free-association technique were posed to the subjects by a male investigator. The questions were worded as follows:

– What are the characteristics required of an educator at the SMP (Department of primary education) for performing his/her task with children? (hereafter referred to as question *Children*).
– What are the characteristics required of an educator at the SMP (Department of primary education) for helping the educational team function? (hereafter referred to as question *Functioning*).

For the student population, the questions did not mention the SMP.

The subjects did not know the content of the second question before answering the first question.

The questions thus revolved around an activity involving children, which is the educator's current assignment or the student's future assignment, and around his/her membership in a work team, which is a major but less often treated pole of his/her work. This choice aimed to induce the individual pole and the group pole respectively in the professional field. The educator's function, while involving taking charge of children, which implies special requirements – being well-balanced, sharing, making decisions and being successful (individual pole) – also becomes explicit within an interdisciplinary work team, which involves abilities to work things out, collaborate with and listen to others (group pole).

The main hypothesis concerned the links between the type of population (students versus workers) and subjects' sex (for more details about the procedure and the hypotheses, see Lorenzi-Cioldi, 1991b). In view of the cultural context of the student milieu which serves as a vehicle for representations favourable to the equality of the sexes, communication and humanism, and condemns, though not always explicitly, sexist or caricatural behaviour and discourses of one or the other sex, we make the following hypothesis.

In students, representations of group and task will not be primarily structured by a stereotypical sex dimension opposing the male instrumental referents to the female expressive referents. These referents will be mixed in the discourse produced by each subject. A plurality of anchorings, competing organizing principles, will thus be at work in this population.

The social context in which educators move differs profoundly from the student milieu. Their working relationships structure their interactions and probably lead them to abandon an egalitarian ideology. Effectiveness may presuppose specialization, hence role differentiation. This social context would be somewhat characterized by representations that are based on the expression of differences and the non-interchangeability of individuals and are fed by collective characteristics. In educators, therefore, we expect to isolate a representational dimension clearly defined by male and female stereotypes. This dimension will be correlated with subjects' sex. Gender – a major organizing principle of representations among practising educators – will then structure in depth their professional activities. By anchoring their representations in the division between males and females, educators will be able to define the specific social functions of their work in terms of sharing their actual experiences with their patients (expressive pole) or programming team activities to achieve their therapeutic aims (instrumental pole).

A Model of Lexical Analysis

The responses collected consisted of short phrases or isolated words. These units of meaning are similar to free associations. Thus, lexical analysis seemed to us better suited and less reductive than thematic analysis.

The responses were submitted to a CFA of textual data. We first built up a data base with all the responses obtained. The analyzed frequency table crossed all the words with individual respondents. Four separate analyses were performed, i.e., an analysis for each population and each of the two questions: *Functioning* and *Children*. As in the classic model of CFA, the results obtained permitted a graphic representation, in the form of factors, of the associations between rows (individuals) and columns (words). The eigenvalues associated with each factor indicated the closeness of the link between these rows and columns. Reading the graphs called for the rules of interpretation mentioned earlier and described non-mathematically by Fénelon (1981), Lorenzi-Cioldi (1983) and Cibois (1983; 1984). Let us recall some basic principles of these rules for the factor analysis of words.

For each analysis performed, a space of words and a space of respondents are calculated. Two words are all the closer in space as they are associated in the representation of several respondents. Similarly, two respondents are close to each other when they use similar words in their responses. Points located around the origin of the factors are read as mean profiles because they do not deviate from the margins of the table. In fact, words do not all have the same weight in the interpretation of a factor. Reading the contributions provides an aid to the interpretation of the solution. We will retain in particular the notion of absolute contribution. Expressed in percentage, it indicates the importance of a given point (word or respondent) in the construction of the factor. The interpretation of factors will be based exclusively on the subsets of words that provide, on a given factor, a larger absolute contribution than the mean contribution.

The Field of Professional Educators

Two CFAs were performed for the responses of thirty-four educators, one for the question *Functioning* and the other for the question *Children*. The latter only will be discussed here. The CFA for the question *Children* included 373 distinct words at the selected frequency threshold.

Figure 12.1 shows the space of the words of CFA of the responses to the question *Children*.

The words positioned near the top of the space of Figure 12.1 (exam-

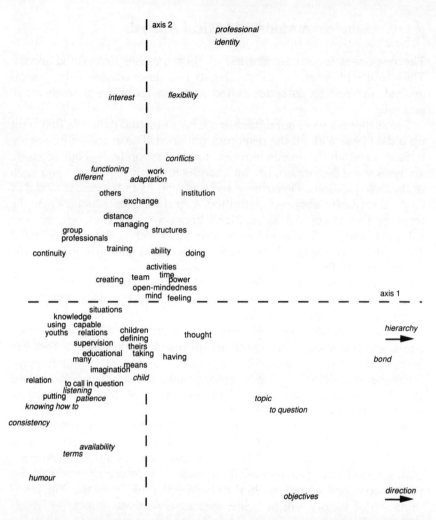

Figure 12.1 *Graphic representation of CFA of the frequency table that intersects words and individuals. Words given in response to the question Children by educators of both sexes.*

Note: Words contributing to factor axes >1.59 are noted in italics.

ples: *professional, identity, conflicts, functioning* and *interest*) are opposed to those placed at its bottom (examples: *humour, availability, question, consistency, patience* and *listening to others*). The opposition between what Parsons and Bales (1955) called the orientations of the male role and those of the female role is clearly at work on the second axis of this analysis. The feelings associated with hierarchy and competition (male stereotype) correspond to desires for relationship, to conscience and to the expression of personal feelings (female stereotype).

The distribution of men and women on this space indicates that men are located mostly near the instrumental or male pole and women near the expressive or female pole (respective means: 0.47 and –0.35; t(32)=2.61; p<0.02).

As for the modal phrases, here are a few examples. For men, *Being able to afford to follow up or implement educational plans, Ability to differentiate oneself from children* and *Defining oneself in terms of scholastic requirements*. For women, *Having a sense of humour, Being available* and *Having an audience*.

The Field of Students

Two CFAs were also performed for the responses of thirty-nine students, one for the question *Functioning*, and the other for the question *Children* (369 words).

Figure 12.2 shows the results obtained for the question *Children*.

Figure 12.2 does not show any differences between the positions of the words relating to sex stereotypicality. On the positive pole of factor 1 are expressive words such as *dialogue* and *question* and instrumental words such as *ability* and *analysis*. On the negative pole of this same factor are expressive words such as *respecting, giving* and *available* and instrumental words such as *ability* and *knowing how to*. On the positive pole of factor 2 are expressive words such as *dialogue* and *available* and instrumental words such as *knowing how to* and *having*. On its negative pole are expressive words such as *respecting* and *contacts* and instrumental words such as *ability* and *taking*.

An examination of the space of respondents shows that the subjects of both sexes are well scattered there. When the means of individual co-ordinates are considered, a slight statistical tendency appears none the less on factor 2 (means: male students = –0.37; female students = 0.07; t(48)=1.82; p<0.10).

As for typical phrases, men used *Listening to others, Feeling like having a good time, Ability to see things in proper perspective so as to last long, Open-mindedness, Articulateness, Analytical ability, Calmness in crises*, while women used *Knowing how to listen to others, Ability to be in authority in certain situations, Knowing how to give a reference framework, Getting to know them perphaps through education, Having a considerable theoretical knowledge of illnesses* and *Knowing oneself and children*.

The results obtained from the student population thus came largely up to our expectations. There were no differences between the representations of both sexes (factor 1), and any slight difference found was not related to the sex stereotypes (factor 2). Their representations seemed to take into account many competing anchorings other than gender.

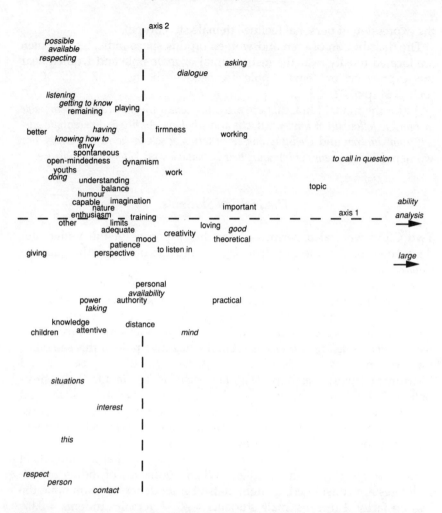

Figure 12.2 *Graphic representation of CFA of the frequency table that intersects words and individuals. Words given in response to the question Children by students of both sexes.*

Note: Words contributing to factor axes >1.54 are noted in italics.

Status of Field Variations

For relating representations to social memberships, there are a set of techniques whose relevance has been illustrated above. The use of such techniques by no means presupposes the existence of a bijection between representations and social memberships. At most, it enables privileged relations to be revealed. A theory of SRs is needed to shed light on the nature of this relationship. Simply using the techniques described in Part Three, however, calls our attention to the existence of sources of variation whose systematism exceeds that of the individual variations studied in the preceding part.

Most of the results reported in this part are compatible with a conception of SRs according to which these variations, either inter-individual or inter-group, are modulations from common organizing principles. It is rare, for instance, that a factor at work in the responses of a group is not found in one way or another in the responses of another group. Of course, it may vary in size, account for more or less of variation or modify itself by incorporating a few different variables. Deciding whether it is a new factor then becomes a question of assessment again. In any event, going through multidimensional analyses serves the better to interpret inter-group differences on specific variables.

Finally, we must not underestimate the indications that seem to demonstrate the existence of group-specific organizations, for example, in the latest research where the 'male-female' dimension intervened in one group, but not in the other.

Conclusion:
Reference Points and Individual Positioning

One major problem in studies on social representations (SRs) is that raw material is composed of collections of individual opinions, attitudes or stereotypes from which the organizing principles common to groups of individuals must be pieced together and linked to their sociological and psychosociological characteristics. In this book we have illustrated the heuristic value of distinguishing three phases in the quantitative analysis of SR.

In a first phase, SRs are objectified through the use of such techniques as cluster analysis, multidimensional scaling or methods of correspondence analysis. In this phase SRs are described as a kind of collective map, common to a given population. Such descriptions constitute a major contribution from statistical analysis, but the study of SRs cannot be stopped when this phase is achieved. Such a limitation would consist in an objectification or reification of SR.

In a second phase, therefore, analytic techniques should deal with the problem of inter-individual differences considered to be variations in individual positioning with respect to common reference points. Showing that social representations are at the same time organizing principles of differences in individual positioning is perhaps the most important contribution of the use of factor analysis and multidimensional scaling analysis of individual differences (INDSCAL).

Phase three focuses on the anchoring of individual variations in sociological and psychosociological characteristics of individuals. We have illustrated the usefulness for that purpose of correspondence analysis with supplementary variables, automatic interaction detection, discriminant analysis and textual data analysis.

In our view social representations are to be defined as principles generating individual positionings that are linked to specific insertions in a set of social relations. They organize the symbolic processes involved in these relations. Data-analysis techniques operationalize well established

154

characteristics of social representations, i.e. objectification and anchoring. But more importantly, the use of various techniques also implies a definition of social representations as organizing principles of differences in individual positioning. What may be consensual in social representations are reference points in relation to which individuals position themselves according to specific social experiences they share with other individuals.

Throughout the book we have evidenced the implications of the use of different data-analysis techniques for a theoretical definition of SR. But we also think that standard uses of these techniques, which do not have their origin in the studies of SR, may now also be seen in a new light.

This is, for instance, true of the famous factors to which factor analysis leads. Debate over their intra-individual nature will not die down any time soon. And even if some well informed authors are still sceptical about its outcome, they do not hesitate to take part in it:

> Perhaps a question on the relation between social structure and intrapersonal structure is unanswerable. One cannot help but wonder, however, whether a certain attitude factor structure found from the responses of many individuals has some sort of representation in the cognitions of individuals. [. . .]. At the very least, we thought, attitude theory and research into the relation between the consensual attitude factors and the cognitive structures of individuals may be encouraged and stimulated. (Kerlinger, 1984, 229)

And this author proved experimentally that propositions highly saturating two factors identified respectively as referring to liberal and conservative representations are better recalled during a memory test than propositions slightly saturating these same factors and this independently of subjects' more or less liberal attitudes. There would therefore be a link between the individual cognitive structure and the structure revealed by the study of inter-individual variations. The existence of such links is also postulated by techniques such as INDSCAL that are of interest when comparing the common structure with the individual structure.

SR studies can feed this debate. While it is true that individuals take a definite position in relation to important issues in a social environment, it is even truer that they must be concerned about the positions of others to organize their interventions and, at least symbolically, take a position in relation to the positions of others. It also turns out that their social memberships are involved in this adoption of reciprocal positions. During a joint physical activity, such as bringing a bulky object into a room, the reciprocal representations of the actions undertaken by different individuals working together do make it easier for them to carry out the task and are doubtless often essential, just as they are essential in more antagonistic relationships. This is even truer for all kinds of more symbolic endeavours that find their reality only in social confrontation and comparison.

If factors exist, it is because there is a symbolic interiorization of this complex interplay of social positioning – interiorization which is always a certain intention to achieve overall co-ordination from one's own viewpoint, more or less shared by the other holders of similar positions. By adopting this idea of organizing principles that are reflected in factor structures, we are not very far from certain ideas of Bourdieu when he referred, for instance, to 'principles of division [that] are common to all the agents of this society and make possible the production of a common and sensible world – a common-sense world' (Bourdieu, 1979, 545–6). Let us recall that for this sociologist, too, common sense was by no means synonymous with consensus. What may be consensual to some extent are endeavours or reference points in relation to which one takes a definite position. Depending on individual positions, however, the relative importance of these reference points may vary, just as the weight of the individual dimensions obtained by INDSCAL varies.

Analytic techniques are often described as inductive. They are used to detect regularities in a multitude of data. At each stage of this approach, however, hypotheses are formulated, if only to choose stimulus words in a free-association task or when defining synonyms for the construction of dictionaries or when choosing the most suitable analysis or during the possible entry of supplementary variables into CFA.

Our use of these methods thus in no way means that we have given up the more deductive method of experimentation, the construction of hypothetico-deductive models and their subsequent illustration in conditions set up for this purpose. Just as Deconchy (1981) showed the limits of a traditional distinction between field and laboratory studies, we are also inclined to downplay the differences between inductive and deductive methods. In fact, a questionnaire-based study, without apparent modification in the social context, may well involve systematic variations by following a rigorous experimental programme.

If we have scarcely dealt with the actual experimental study of SRs, it is not for lack of material or interest. In fact, each of us has made full use of this method to study SRs, sometimes by combining it with factor-analysis methods (see especially Lorenzi-Cioldi, 1988a). Even if experimenters do not directly use these methods, they often employ tools such as attitude scales that are the product of factor analysis. In this book, however, we have tried to stick as closely as possible to the most commonly used methods of these analyses.

It is hoped that this choice has had the merit of focusing the reader's attention on what is specific to these methods. It has, perhaps, had a drawback. In fact, as such, these methods do not deal with dynamics of change, even if they can be used to compare 'different states' of a representation as done by Paicheler and Beaufils (in press) by reanalyzing two sets of findings by Maisonneuve (1979) after an interval of twenty years. It is still true, however, that the experimental method, working on contents validated by the contribution of other analytic methods, seems to us particularly well suited for showing that regularities detected by these analyses should not be considered to be reified entities. Experimentation may create situational dynamics that modify SRs and illustrate how a change in the metasystem of social regulations modifies relevant representations in a situation.

This book dealt with the quantitative analysis of SR. Readers familiar with the literature on SRs know that, from the beginning of their study by French authors such as Moscovici (1961, 1976), Herzlich (1973), Chombart de Lauwe (1984), Jodelet (1991), study of SR has heavily relied on what is now called discourse analysis (Potter and Wetherell, 1987). The concepts of objectification and anchoring were forged to account for characteristics of discourse as produced in interviews, newspapers or novels. They remain useful for studying aspects of SR that are produced in social interactions that take place when respondents fill in questionnaires in more or less standardized conditions. But techniques used for such studies imply also a definition of SR as principles that generate individual positioning linked to specific insertions in sets of social relationships. This is perhaps the most important result of the use of quantitative data-analysis techniques in the study of SR.

Bibliography

Abric, J.C., Vacherot, G. (1976), 'Méthodologie et étude expérimentale des représentations sociales: tâche, partenaire et comportement en situation de jeu', *Bulletin de psychologie*, **29**, 63–71.

Aldenderfer, M.S., Blashfield, R.K. (1985), *Cluster Analysis* (London: Sage, Quantitative applications in the social sciences no. 44).

Aldrovanti, M., Beauvois, J.L., Guingouin, G. (1987), 'Théories implicites de la personnalité, travail cognitif, et idéologie', *in* J.L. Beauvois, R.-V. Joule, J.-M. Monteil, *Perspectives cognitives et conduites sociales* (Fribourg: DelVal).

Arabie, P., Carroll, J.D., DeSarbo, W.S. (1987), *Three-way Scaling and Clustering* (London: Sage).

Augoustinos, M., Innes, J.M. (1990), 'Towards an integration of social representations and social schema theory', *British Journal of Social Psychology*, **29**, 213–31.

Bacher, F. (1982), *Les Enquêtes en psychologie*, 2 vols (Lille: Presses Universitaires).

Beauvois, J.L. (1982), 'Théories implicites de la personnalité, évaluation et reproduction idéologique', *L'Année psychologique*, **82**, 513–36.

Beauvois, J.L. (1984), *La Psychologie quotidienne* (Paris: Presses Universitaires de France).

Beauvois, J. L., Roulin, J. L., Tiberghien, G. (1990), *Manuel d'etudes pratiques de psychologie. I. Pratique de la recherche* (Paris: Presses Universitaires de France).

Bellelli, G. (1987), *La Représentation sociale de la maladie mentale* (Napoli: Liguori).

Bem, S. (1974), 'The measurement of psychological androgyny', *Journal of Consulting and Clinical Psychology*, **42**, 155–62.

Bernstein, B. (1975), *Langage et classes sociales* (Paris: Editions de Minuit).

Béroud, G., Clémence, A., Meyer, G. (1985), 'Les apprentis: Images de soi et images du monde', *Revue suisse de sociologie*, **11**, 61–90.

Bisseret, N. (1974), 'Langage et identité de classe: Les classes sociales "se" parlent', *L'Année sociologique*, **25**, 237–64.

Boltanski, L. (1984), 'La dénonciation', *Actes de la recherche en sciences sociales*, **51**, 3–40.

Bourdieu, P. (1977), 'L'économie des échanges linguistiques', *Langue française*, **34**, 17–34.

Bourdieu, P. (1979), *La distinction, critique sociale du jugement* (Paris: Editions de Minuit).

Burton, M. (1972), 'Semantic dimensions of occupation names', *in* A.K. Romney, R.N. Shepard, S. B. Nerlove (eds), *Multidimensional Scaling. Theory and applications in the behavioral sciences*, Vol. II (New York: Seminar Press).

Carroll, J.D., Chang, J.J. (1970), 'Analysis of individual differences in multidimensional scaling via an N-way generalization of "Eckart-Young" decomposition', *Psychometrika*, **35**, 283–319.

Carroll R.M., Field J. (1974), 'A comparison of the classification accuracy of profile similarity measures', *Multivariate Behavioral Research*, **9**, 373–80.

Cattell, R.B. (1944), 'Psychological measurement: Normative, ipsative, interactive', *Psychological Review*, **51**, 292–303.

Chombart de Lauwe, M.J. (1984), 'Changes in the representation of the child in the course of social transmission', *in* R. M. Farr, S. Moscovici (eds), *Social Representations* (Cambridge: Cambridge University Press, 185–209).

Cibois, P. (1983), *L'Analyse factorielle* (Paris: Presses Universitaires de France).

Cibois, P. (1984), *L'Analyse des données en sociologie* (Paris: Presses Universitaires de France).

Clémence, A., Deschamps, J. C., Roux, P. (1986), 'La Perception de l'entrée en apprentissage', *L'Orientation scolaire et professionnelle*, **15**, 311–30.

Codol, J.-P. (1986), 'Estimation et expression de la ressemblance et de la différence entre pairs', *L'Année psychologique*, **86**, 527–50.

Comrey, A.L. (1978), 'Common methodological problems in factor analytic studies', *Journal of Consulting and Clinical Psychology*, **46**, 648–59.

Costermans, J. (1979), 'Exploration de structures cognitives lexicalisées par une épreuve de combinaison syntagmatique', *Cahiers de l'Institut de Linguistique de Louvain*, **51**, 61–79.

Coxon, A.P.M. (1982), *The User's Guide to Multidimensional Scaling* (London: Heinemann Educational Books).

Coxon, A.P.M., Davies, P.M. (1986), *Images of Social Stratification: Occupational structures and class* (London: Sage).

Deconchy, J. P. (1981), 'Laboratory experimentation and social field experimentation: An ambiguous distinction', *European Journal of Social Psychology*, **11**, 323–47.

Degenne, A., Vergès, P. (1973), 'Introduction à l'analyse de similitude', *Revue française de sociologie*, **14**, 471–512.

De Paolis, P., Lorenzi-Cioldi, F., Pombeni, M.L. (1983), 'Il Lavoro dello psicologo: L'Immagine di un gruppo di studenti di psicologia', *Giornali di psicologia*, **1**, 143–61.

De Polo, M., Sarchielli, G. (1983), 'Le Rappresentazioni sociali del lavoro', *Giornale di psicologia*, **3**, 501–19.

De Rosa, A. S. (1987), 'Différents Niveaux d'analyse du concept de représentation sociale en relation aux méthodes utilisées', *in* G. Bellelli (ed.), *La Représentation sociale de la maladie mentale* (Napoli: Liguori, 47–63).

De Rosa, A.S. (1988), 'Sur l'Usage des associations libres dans l'étude des représentations sociales de la maladie mentale', *Connexions*, **51**, 27–50.

Deschamps, J.C., Clémence, A. (1987), *L'Explication quotidienne*. (Cousset: Delval).

Deschamps, J.C., Lorenzi-Cioldi, F., Meyer, G. (1982), *L'Echec scolaire. Elève modèle ou modèles d'élève?* (Lausanne: Editions Pierre-Marcel Favre).

Di Giacomo, J.P. (1980), 'Intergroup alliances and rejections within a protest movement', *European Journal of Social Psychology*, **10**, 329–44.

Di Giacomo J.P. (1987), 'Fonction sociale et individuelle des représentations sociales', *in* G. Bellelli (ed.), *La Représentation sociale de la maladie mentale*, (Napoli: Liguori, 65–74).

Doise, W. (1985), 'Représentations sociales chez des élèves: Effets du statut scolaire et de l'origine sociale', *Revue suisse de psychologie*, **44**, 67–78.

Doise, W. (1986), 'Les représentations sociales: Définition d'un concept', *in* W. Doise, A. Palmonari (eds), *L'Etude des représentations sociales*, (Paris: Delachaux & Niestlé, 81–94).

Doise, W. (1989a), 'Attitudes et représentations sociales' *in* D. Jodelet (ed.), *Les Représentations sociales* (Paris: Presses Universitaires de France, 220–38).

Doise, W. (1989b), 'Cognitions et représentations sociales: l'Approche génétique', *in* D. Jodelet (ed.), *Les Représentations sociales* (Paris: Presses Universitaires de France, 341–62).

Doise, W. (1990), 'Les Représentations sociales', *in* R. Ghiglione, C. Bonnet, J.F. Richard (eds), *Traité de psychologie cognitive 3: Cognition, représentation, communication* (Paris: Dunod, 111–74).

Doise, W., Lorenzi-Cioldi, F. (1991), 'L'Identité comme représentation sociale', *in* J.-P. Deconchy (ed.), *Idéologie et représentations sociales* (Cousset (CH): Delval).

Doise, W., Mugny, G., De Paolis, P., Kaiser, C., Lorenzi-Cioldi, F. and Papastamou, S. (1982), 'Présentation d'un questionnaire sur les psychologues', *Bulletin suisse des psychologues*, **3**, 189–206.

Doise W., Papastamou S., (1987), 'Représentations sociales des causes de la délinquance: Croyances générales et cas concrets', *Déviance et société*, **11**, 153–62.

Espéret, E. (1979), *Langage et origine sociale des elèves* (Berne: Peter Lang).

Fénelon, J. P. (1981) *Qu'est-ce que l'Analyse des données?*, (Paris: Lefonen).

Flament, C. (1986), 'L'Analyse de similitude: Une Technique pour les recherches sur les représentations sociales', *in* W. Doise, A. Palmonari (eds), *L'Etude des représentations sociales* (Paris: Delachaux & Niestlé, 139–56).

Francès, R. (1980), *L'Idéologie dans l'université* (Paris: Presses Universitaires de France).

Funck, S.G., Horowitz, A.D., Lipshitz, R., Young, F.W. (1976), 'The perceived structure of American ethnic groups: The use of multidimensional scaling in stereotype research', *Sociometry*, **39**, 116–30.

Galli, I., Nigro G. (1986), 'La Rappresentazione sociale del potere in un campione di studenti universitari. La Trama primitiva', *Psicologia e societa*, **1**, 20-31.

Gärlin, T. (1976), 'A multidimensional scaling and semantic differential technique study of the perception of environmental settings', *Scandinavian Journal of Psychology*, **17**, 323–32.

Gilly, M. (1972), 'La Représentation de l'élève par le maître a l'école primaire. Cohérence entre aspects structuraux et différentiels', *Cahiers de psychologie*, 1972, **15**, 201–16.

Guilford, J.P. (1952), 'When not to factor analyze', *Psychological Bulletin*, **49**, 26–37.

Guimelli, C. (1989), 'Pratiques nouvelles et transformation sans rupture d'une représentation sociale: La Représentation de la chasse et de la nature', *in* J. L. Beauvois, R. V. Joule, J. M. Monteil (eds), *Perspectives cognitives et conduites sociales 2. Représentations et processus socio-cognitifs* (Cousset: Delval, 117–38).

Guttman, L. (1944), 'A basis for scaling quantitative data', *American Sociological Review*, 9, 139–50.

Heise, D.R. (1970), 'The semantic differential and attitude research', *in* G.F. Summers (ed.), *Attitude Measurement* (Chicago: Rand McNally).

Herzlich, C. (1973), *Health and Illness: A social psychological analysis* (London: Academic Press).

Hudson, H.C. (1982), *Classifying Social Data* (San Francisco: Jossey-Bas).

Huteau, M. (1976), *Les Représentations professionnelles des adolescents* (Paris: Laboratoire de Psychologie Différentielle).

Jodelet, D. (1989), *Les Représentations sociales* (Paris: Presses Universitaires de France).

Jodelet, D. (1991), *Madness and Social Representations* (Hemel Hempstead: Harvester Wheatsheaf).

Johnson, R.L., Wall, D.D. (1969), 'Cluster analysis of semantic differential data', *Educational and Psychological Measurement*, **29**, 769–80.

Katz, D., Braly, K. W. (1933), 'Racial stereotypes of 100 college students', *Journal of Abnormal and Social Psychology*, **28**, 280–90.

Kerlinger, F.N. (1984), *Liberalism and Conservatism: The nature and structure of social attitudes* (Hillsdale: Lawrence Erlbaum).

Kruskal, J.B. (1964), 'Multidimensional scaling: A numerical method', *Psychometrika*, **29**, 1–27.

Kruskal, J.B., Wish, M. (1976), *Multidimensional Scaling* (London: Sage, Quantitative Applications in the Social Sciences no. 11).

Kuhn, M. H., McPartland, T. S. (1955), 'An empirical investigation of self-attitude', *American Sociological Review*, **19**, 68–76.

Le Bouedec, G. (1984), 'Contribution à la méthodologie d'étude des représentations sociales', *Cahiers de psychologie cognitive*, **4**, 245–72.

Le Poultier, F. (1986), *Travail social, inadaptation sociale et processus cognitifs* (Vanves: Centre Technique National d'Etudes et de Recherches sur les Handicapés et les Inadaptations).

Leyens, J. Ph. (1983), *Sommes-nous tous des psychologues?* (Bruxelles: Pierre Mardaga).

Likert, R. (1932), 'A technique for the measurement of attitudes', *Archives of Psychology*, whole no. 140.

Lorenzi-Cioldi, F. (1983), 'L'Analyse factorielle des correspondances dans les sciences sociales', *Revue suisse de sociologie*, **9**, 365–90.

Lorenzi-Cioldi, F. (1988a), *Individus dominants et groupes dominés* (Grenoble: Presses Universitaires).

Lorenzi-Cioldi, F. (1988b), 'Déterminants de l'actualisation du schème de catégorisation sexuelle', *in* CREPCO (Université de Provence, ed.), *Construction et fonctionnement de l'identité* (Aix-en-Provence: Centre de Recherche en Psychologie Cognitive, 327–36).

Lorenzi-Cioldi, F. (1991a), 'Self-stereotyping and self-enhancement in gender groups', *European Journal of Social Psychology*, **21**, 403–17.

Lorenzi-Cioldi, F. (1991b), 'Pluralité d'ancrages des représentations professionnelles chez des éducateurs en formation et des praticiens', *Revue internationale de psychologie sociale*, **4**, 357–79.

Lorenzi-Cioldi, F., Joye, D. (1988), 'Représentations sociales de catégories socioprofessionnelles: Aspects méthodologiques', *Bulletin de psychologie*, **61**, 377–90.

Lorenzi-Cioldi, F., Meyer, G. (1984), *Semblables ou différents: Identité sociale et représentations collectives de jeunes immigrés dans le contexte scolaire genevois* (Genève: Bureau International du Travail).

Maisonneuve, J. (1979), *Recherches diachroniques sur une représentation sociale* (Paris: Editions du C.N.R.S.).

Manz, W. (1968), *Das Stereotyp* (Meisenheim am Glan: Verlag Anton Hain).

Marques, J.M., Yzerbyt, V.Y., Leyens, J.-P. (1988), 'The "black sheep effect": Extremity of judgments towards ingroup members as a function of group identification', *European Journal of Social Psychology*, **18**, 1–16.

Monteil, J.-M., Mailhot, L. (1988), 'Eléments d'une représentation sociale de la formation: Analyse d'une enquête auprès d'une population de formateurs', *Connexions*, **51**, 9–26.

Moscovici, S. (1961), *La Psychanalyse, son image et son public* (Paris: Presses Universitaires de France, 2nd edn, 1976).

Moscovici, S. (1986), 'L'Ere des représentations sociales', *in* W. Doise, A. Palmonari (eds), *L'Etude des représentations sociales* (Neuchâtel: Delachaux & Niestlé).

Moscovici, S., Hewstone, M. (1984), 'De la Science au sens commun', *in* S. Moscovici (ed.), *Psychologie sociale* (Paris: Presses Universitaires de France, 539–66).

Mugny, G., Carugati, F. (1989), *Social Representations of Intelligence* (London and Paris: Cambridge University Press and Maison des Sciences de l'Homme).

Nisbett, R. E., Ross, L. (1980), *Human Inference: Strategies and shortcomings of social judgment* (Englewood Cliffs, NJ: Prentice Hall).

Osgood, C.E., Suci, G.J., Tannenbaum, P.H. (1957), *The Measurement of Meaning* (Urbana: University of Illinois Press, 1957).

Paicheler, H. (1984), 'L'Epistémologie du sens commun', *in* S. Moscovici (ed.), *Psychologie sociale* (Paris: Presses Universitaires de France, 277–307).

Paicheler, H., Beaufils, B. (in press), 'Théories implicites de la personnalité et représentations sociales'.

Palmonari, A. (1981), *Psicologi* (Bologne: Il Mulino).

Palmonari, A., Zani, B. (1989), 'Les Représentations sociales dans le champ des professions psychologiques', *in* D. Jodelet (ed.), *Les Représentations sociales* (Paris: Presses Universitaires de France).

Parsons, T., Bales R.F. (1955), *Family, Socialization, and Interaction Processes* (New York: Free Press).

Peabody, D. (1968), 'Group judgements in the Philippines: Evaluative and descriptive aspects', *Journal of Personality and Social Psychology*, **10**, 290–300.

Peabody, D. (1985), *National Characteristics* (Cambridge: Cambridge University Press).

Pedhazur, E. (1982), *Multiple Regression in Behavioral Research: Explanation and prediction* (New York: Holt, Rinehart & Winston).

Potter, J., Wetherell, M. (1987), *Discourse and Social Psychology* (London: Sage).

Poulton, E.C. (1989), *Bias in Quantifying Judgments* (Hillsdale, NJ: Lawrence Erlbaum).

Roqueplo, P. (1974), *Le Partage du savoir* (Paris: Editions du Seuil).

Rosenberg, S. (1988), 'Self and others: Studies in social personality and autobiography', *in* L. Berkowitz (ed.), *Advances in Social Psychology*, Vol. 21 (London: Academic Press).

Rosenberg, S., Nelson, L., Vivekananthan, P. S. (1968), 'A multidimensional approach to the structure of personality impressions', *Journal of Personality and Social Psychology*, **9**, 283–94.

Rosenberg, S., Olshan, K. (1970), 'Evaluative and descriptive aspects in personality perception', *Journal of Personality and Social Psychology*, **16**, 619–26.

Rosenberg, S., Sedlack, A. (1972), 'Structural representations of perceived trait relationships', *in* A.K. Romney, R.N. Shepard, S.B. Nerlove (eds), *Multidimensional Scaling. Theory and applications in the behavioral sciences,*. Vol. II (New York: Seminar Press).

Rummel, R. J. (1974), *Applied Factor Analysis* (Evanston: Northwestern University Press).

Salmaso, P., Pombeni, L. (1986), 'Le concept de travail', *in* W. Doise, A. Palmonari (eds), *L'Etude des representations sociales* (Paris: Delachaux & Niestlé, 196–207).

Semin, G.R. (1987), 'On the relationship between representation of theories in psychology and ordinary language', *in* W. Doise, S. Moscovici (eds), *Current Issues in European Social Psychology*, Volume 2 (Cambridge: Cambridge University Press, 307–48).

Semin G.R., Chassein, J. (1985), 'The relationship between higher order models and everyday conceptions of personality', *European Journal of Social Psychology*, **15**, 1–15.

Shiffman, S.S., Reynolds, M.L., Young, F.W. (1981), *Introduction to Multidimensional Scaling: Theory, methods, and applications* (London: Academic Press).

Summers, G. E. (1970), *Attitude Measurement* (Chicago: Rand MacNally).

Thomas, W.I., Znaniecki (1918–20), *The Polish Peasant in Europe and America*, 2 vols (Chicago: University of Chicago Press).

Thurstone, L.L. (1955), *L'analyse factorielle et ses applications* (Paris: Editions du Centre National de la Recherche Scientifique).

Thurstone, L.L., Chave, E.J. (1929), *The Measurement of Attitude* (Chicago: University of Chicago Press).

Verquerre, R. (1989), *Représentations de l'enfant, attitudes educatives, comportements educatifs* (Université Paris 5: Thèse de Doctorat d'Etat).

Wish, M. (1976), 'Comparisons among multidimensional structures of interpersonal relations', *Multivariate Behavioral Research*, **11**, 297–324.

Wish, M., Deutsch, M., Biener, L. (1970), 'Differences in conceptual structures of nations: An explanatory study', *Journal of Personality and Social Psychology*, **16**, 361–73.

Wish, M., Deutsch, M., Kaplan, S.J. (1976), 'Perceived dimensions of interpersonal relations', *Journal of Personality and Social Psychology*, **33**, 409–20.

Zani, B. (in press), 'Social representations of mental illness: Naives and professional perspectives', *in* G. Breakwell, D. Canter (eds), *Empirical Approaches to Social Representations* (Oxford: Oxford University Press).

Subject Index

Author Index